JOURNEYS

Practice Book

Volume 1

Grade 1

Printed in the U.S.A.

ISBN 10: 0-54-724641-2
ISBN 13: 978-0-54-724641-3

16 17 18 0982 16 15 14
4500457049

Contents

Name ______________________

Listen for the Short *a* and *m* Sounds

Say each picture name. Listen for the short a sound. Write the letter a to show where you hear the short a sound.

1.

2.

3.

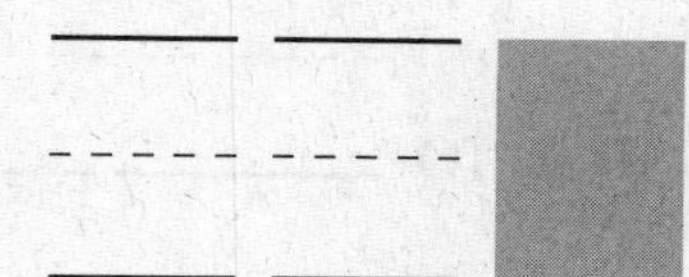

Say each picture name. Listen for the *m* sound. Write the letter **m** to show where you hear the sound for **m**.

4.

5.

6.

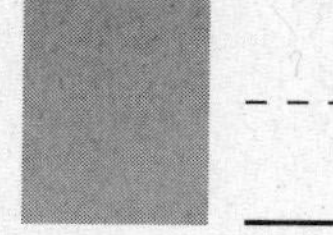

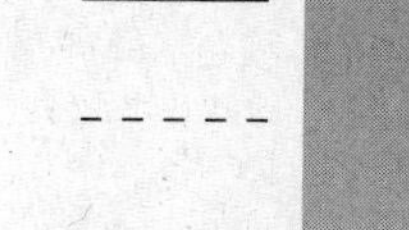

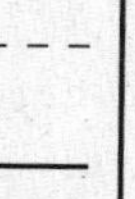

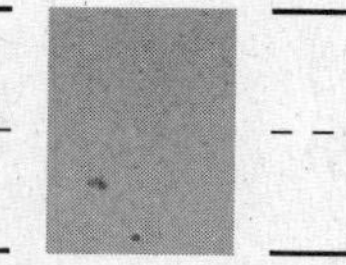

Name ______________________________

Words to Know

Read the words in the box. Then read and finish the sentences.

Words to Know

am I to like

I am ______________________.

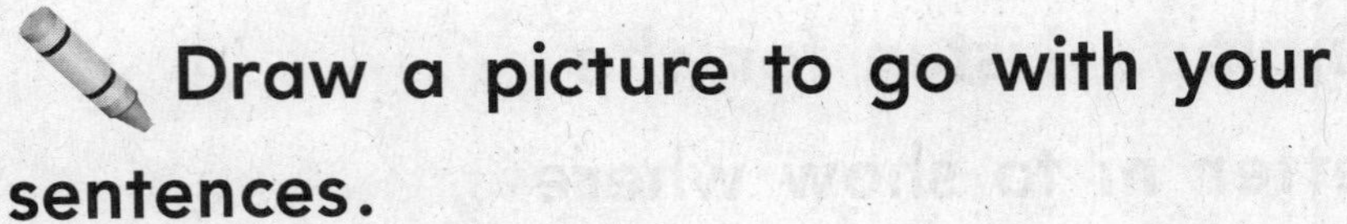

I like to ______________________.

Draw a picture to go with your sentences.

Name ______________________________

Listen for the *s*, *m*, and Short *a* Sounds

Say each picture name. Listen for the /s/ sound. Write the letter **s** to show where you hear the sound for **s**.

1.

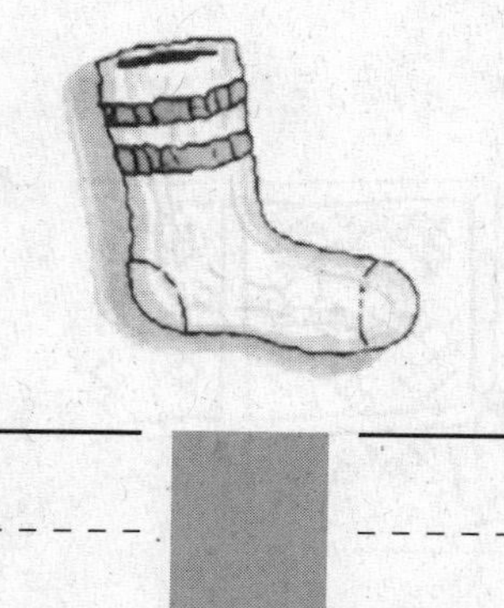

2.

3.

Listen to each picture name. Listen for the sounds. Use the letters **s**, **a**, or **m** to write the picture name. Remember that a person's name begins with a capital letter.

4.

___ ___ t

5.

___ ___ d

6.

Name ____________________

Back to School
PRACTICE BOOK

High-Frequency Words

Words to Know

Read the words in the box. Then read the story.

Words to Know

a see the I to like

I am Sam.

I see a .

I like the .

I see a .

I like the .

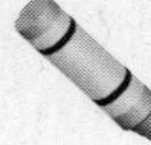

Draw what will happen next in the story.

Name ___________________________________

Back to School
PRACTICE BOOK

Phonics

Listen for the *t*, *s*, *m*, and Short *a* Sounds

Say each picture name. Listen for the *t* sound. Write the letter **t** to show where you hear the sound for **t**.

1. ___ ___

2. ___ ___

3. ___ ___

Listen to each picture name. Listen for the sounds. Use the letters **t**, **s**, **a**, or **m** to write the name.

4. ___ ___ p

5. ___ ___ ___

6. ___ ___ ___

Name ____________________

Words to Know

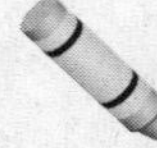

Read the words in the box. Then read the story. Draw a line under the words that have short a.

Words to Know

we go I a see like to the

I am Tam.
I am Sam.
We see a mat.
We like the mat.
We go to the mat.

Draw what Sam and Tam will do next.

Name ____________________

Listen for the *c*, *t*, *m*, and Short *a* Sounds

Say each picture name. Listen for the sounds in the name. Color the pictures that begin with the same sound as **cat**.

1.

Listen to each picture name. Listen for the sounds. Use the letters **c**, **t**, **a**, or **m** to write the picture name.

2. ___ ___ ___
___ ___ p

3. ___ ___ ___
___ ___ n

4. ___ ___ ___
___ ___ ___

Name ______________________________

Words to Know

Read the words in the box. Then read the story. Draw a line under the words that have short a.

Words to Know

is are we go I a see like to the

We see Sam.
Sam is the cat.
Am I a cat?
Is Cam a cat?
We are the 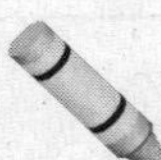 .
We like Sam.
We go to see Sam!

Draw what will happen next in the story.

Name ______________________

Letters and Sounds

 Trace and read the words. Draw a line from each word to its picture.

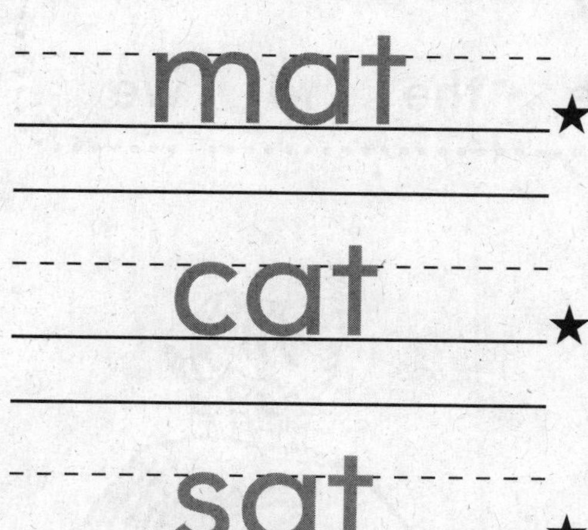

mat ★

cat ★

sat ★

★ 

★ 

★ 

 Circle the words that rhyme with at.

at	cat	Tam	mat
Cam	Sam	am	sat

Name ___________________________

Words to Know

Read the words in the box. Then read the story.

Words to Know

a are go I like is see the to we

We are at the zoo.

We see a cat.

The cat is a tiger.

I like the cat.

We like to go to the zoo.

Think about places that you like to visit. Write about and draw your ideas.

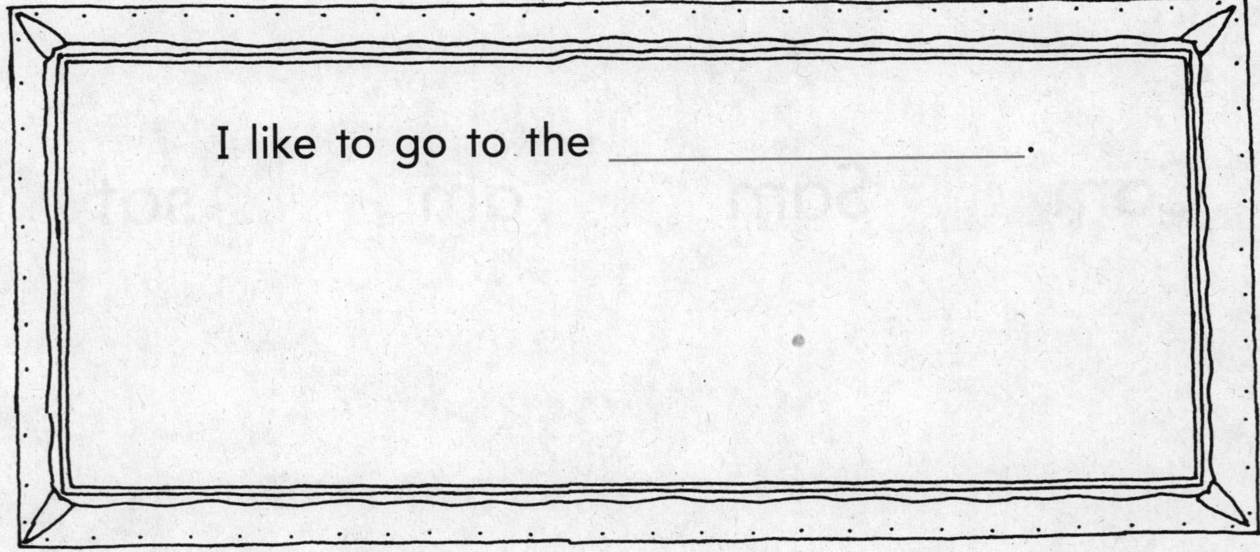

Name ________________________________

Words to Know

Complete the sentences. Write a word from the box on each line.

Words to Know

with help and you play be

1. Look at Cam ____________ Sam.

2. What will this ____________ ?

3. I like to ____________ .

4. She can ____________ .

5. Come ____________ me, Sam!

6. ____________ can go down.

Name ______________________

What Is a Pal?
Phonics: Short *a*

Words with Short *a*

Write the missing letter. Read the word.

1. 

___ a t

2. 

___ a t

3. 

D ___ n

4. 

c ___ t

5. 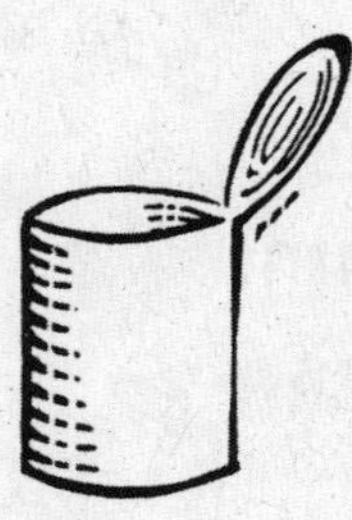

___ a n

6. 

S ___ m

Name ____________________

What Is a Pal?
Phonics: Consonants *s, n, d*

Consonants *s, n, d*

Name each picture. Think of the beginning sound. Write s, n, or d.

1.

2.

3.

4.

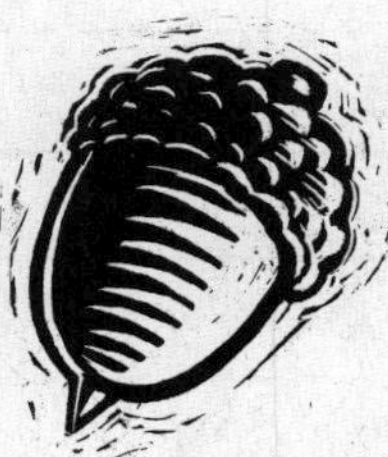

5.

6.

Name ____________________

Spelling Words with the Short *a* Sound

Sort the words. Write the correct Spelling Words in each column.

Words that have 2 letters	Words that have 3 letters

Spelling Words

am
at
sat
man
dad
mat

Name ______________________

Nouns for People

Listen to the nouns in the Word Bank. Read along. Write nouns from the box to name the people in the picture.

Word Bank

Pam
fireman
grandma
dad

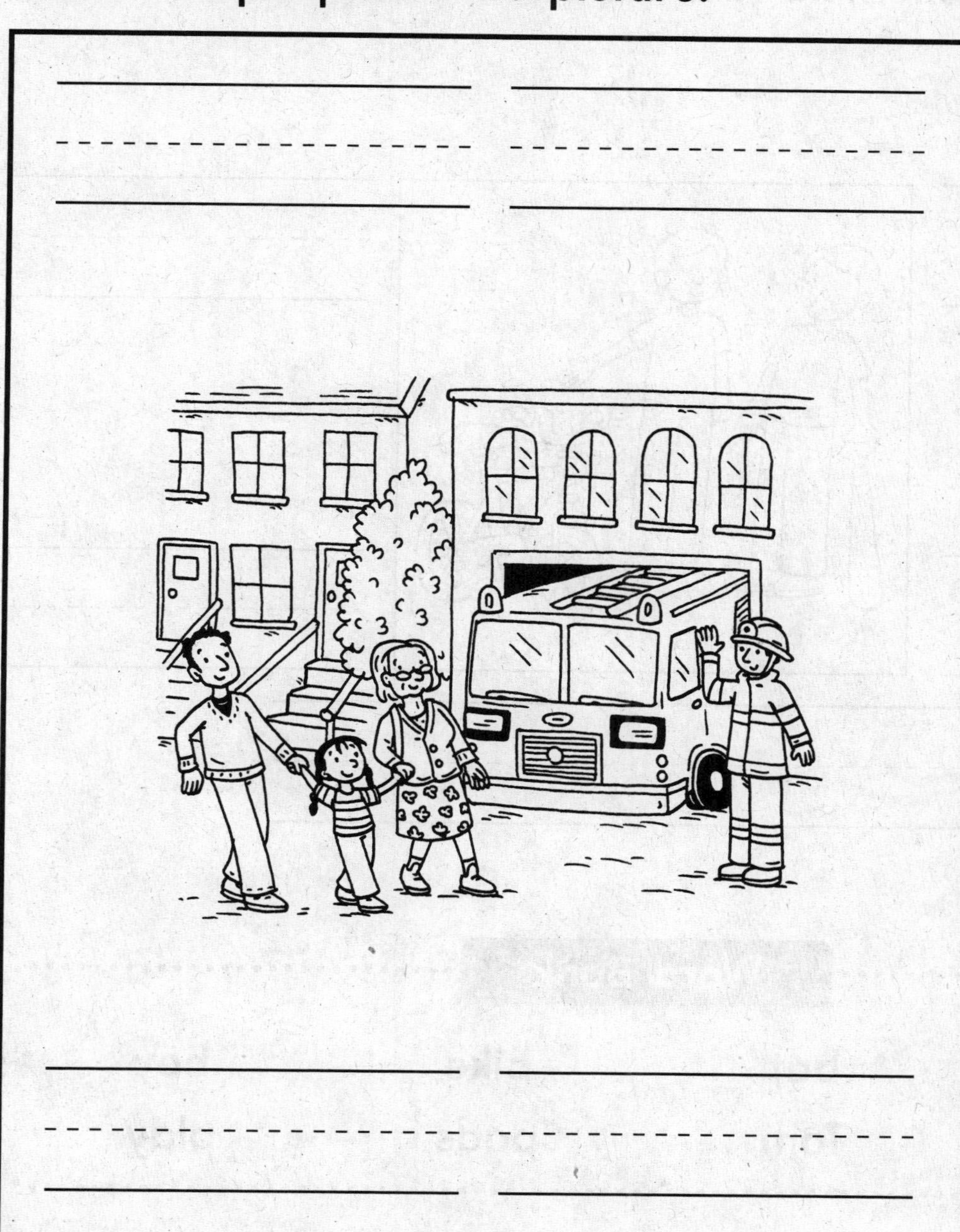

Name ______________________________

What Is a Pal?
Writing: Writing About Us

Giving Details

Listen to the words in the Word Bank. Read along. Add two details to this picture of two pals. Then write labels that tell who and what.

Word Bank

cap	bat	bike	boy
Sam	Tom	pads	play

Name ________________________________

Consonants *p, f*

Name each picture. Think of the beginning sound. Write **p** or **f**.

1.

2.
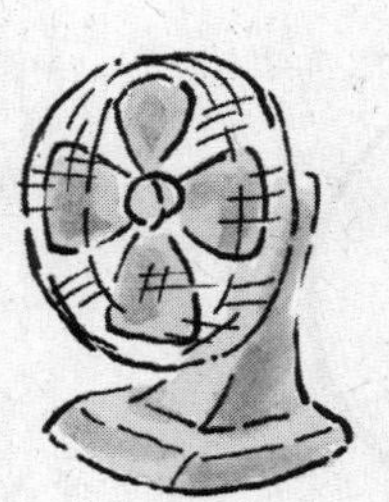

3.

4.
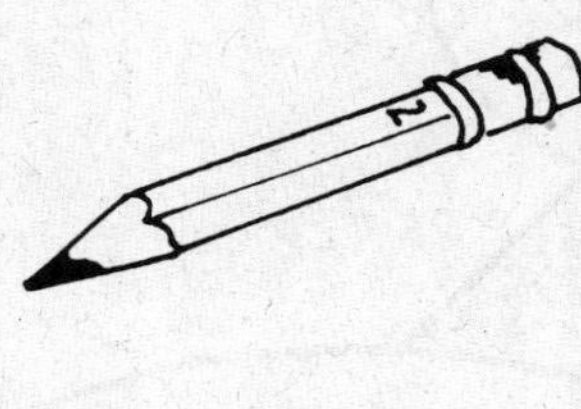

5.

6.

7.
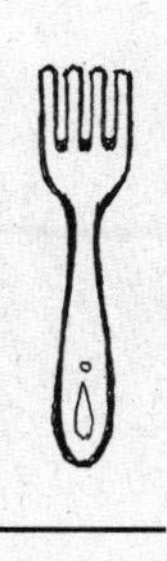

8.
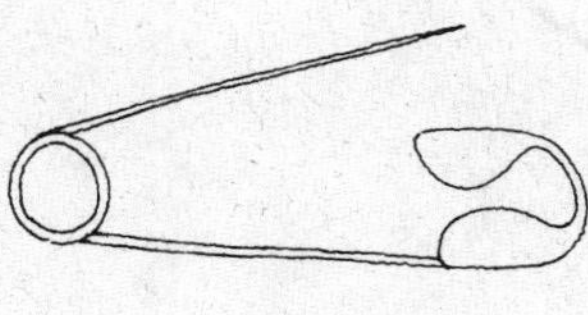

9.

Name ______________________________

What Is a Pal?
Comprehension: Main Idea

Main Idea

The story is about pals. Write things from the story that tell about pals.

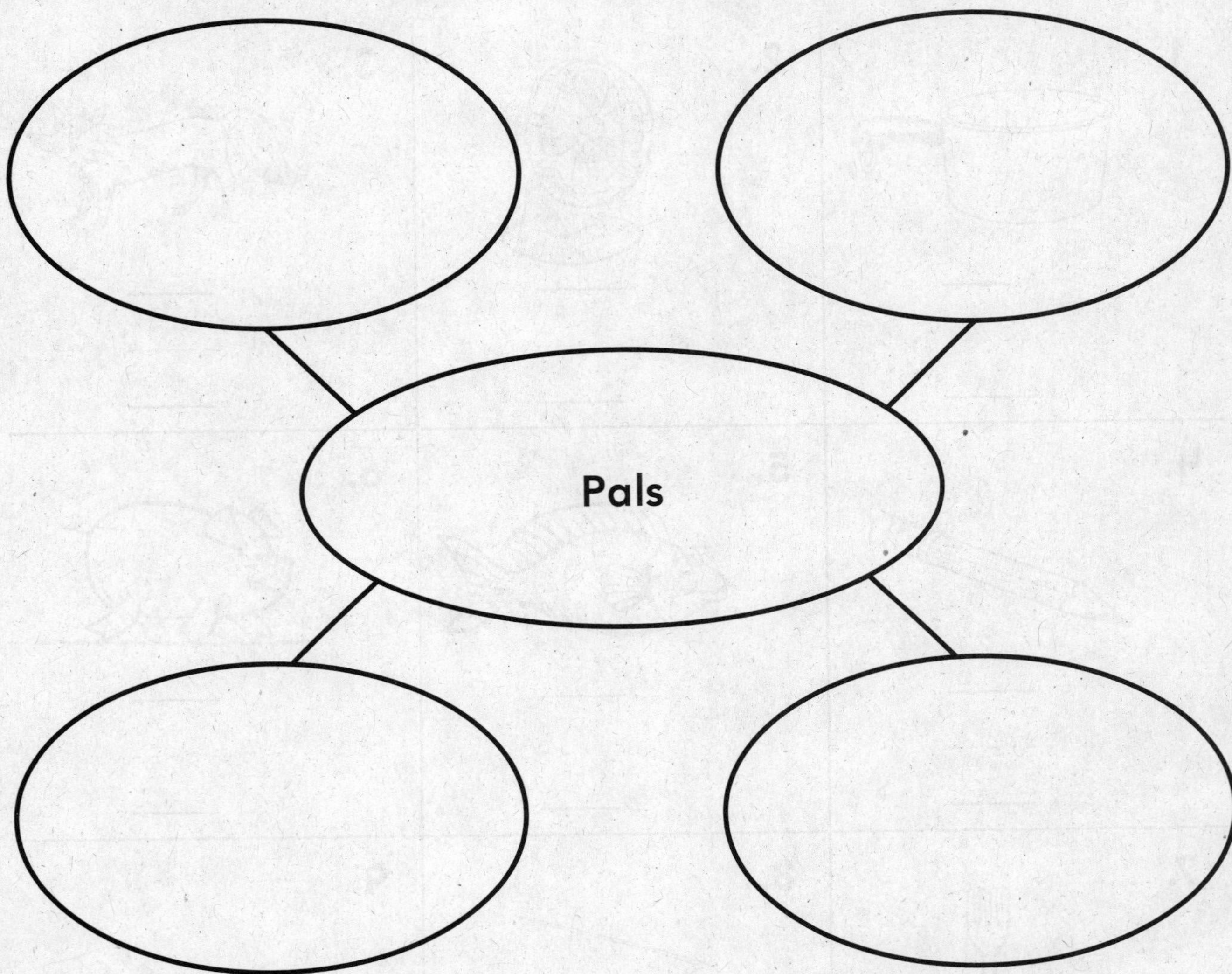

Name ______________________________

Spelling Words with the Short *a* Sound

Spelling Words

- am
- at
- sat
- man
- dad
- mat

Write the missing letter to complete each Spelling Word. Then write the word.

1. s ___ t ______________
2. m ___ n ______________
3. m ___ t ______________
4. ___ t ______________
5. d ___ d ______________
6. ___ m ______________

Name ______________________________

What Is a Pal?
Grammar: Nouns

Words That Name Animals

Listen to the nouns in the Word Bank. Read along. Write a noun from the box to name each picture.

Word Bank

mouse
bird
dog
cat
bear

1.  ______________________________

2.  ______________________________

3.  ______________________________

4.  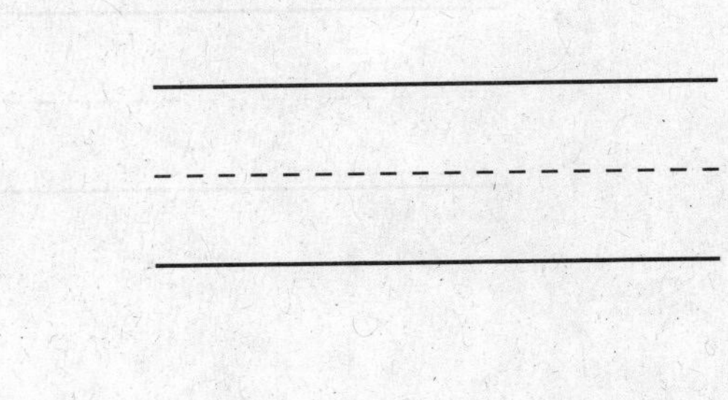 ______________________________

5.  ______________________________

Name ____________________

My Pals

What Is a Pal?
Writing: Writing About Us

Draw four pals. Show details that tell who and what.

My Pals

Write labels for your pictures.

Name ______________________________

Spelling Words with the Short *a* Sound

Write the correct word to complete each sentence.

1. This ______________ is for the cat. (mat, dad)

2. I ______________ with it. (dad, sat)

3. I ______________ mad. (mat, am)

4. Pat is ______________ the play. (at, am)

5. We like the ______________. (man, at)

6. We sat on ______________. (at, dad)

Name ____

Spiral Review

Circle the correct word in each box to name each person and pet.

1.		sam / Sam al / Al
2.		Sal / sal Gam / gam
3.		dan / Dan cal / Cal
4.		Cam / cam Mag / mag

Name ___________________________

What Is a Pal?
Grammar: Nouns for People and Animals

Grammar in Writing

Words that name people and animals are called **nouns**. Use nouns to name people and animals when you write.

The boy smiles.
The dog runs.

Listen to the nouns in the Word Bank, and to the sentences. Read along. Look at the picture. Write nouns from the box to finish the sentences.

Word Bank
dad
girl
cat
boy

1. The ____________ plays.
2. The ____________ cooks.
3. The ____________ helps.
4. The ____________ sleeps.

Name ______________________

Words to Know

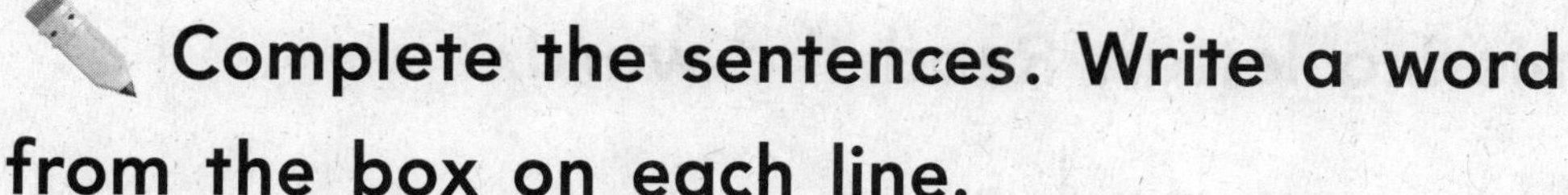

Complete the sentences. Write a word from the box on each line.

Words to Know					
he	look	have	too	for	what

1. I will ______________ for the cat.

2. ______________ is a good cat.

3. My dad will look, ______________ .

4. He will help me look ______________ the cat.

5. ______________ is this?

6. I ______________ the cat!

Name ______________________

Words with Short *i*

Write the missing letter. Read the word.

1.

s ___ t

2.

T ___ m

3.

p ___ n

4.

f ___ n

5.

s ___ p

6.

h ___ t

Name ______________________

Consonants *r, h, /z/s*

Write the missing letter. Read the word.

1.

___ a m

2.

h i ___

3.

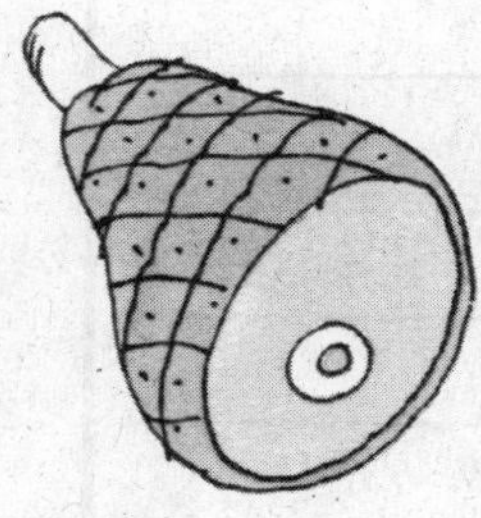

___ a m

4.

___ a n

5.

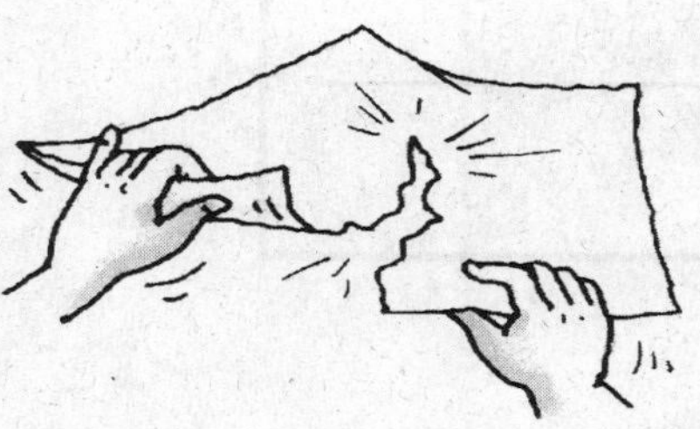

___ i p

6.

___ a t

Name ______________________________

Spelling Words with the Short *i* Sound

Sort the words. Write the correct Spelling Words in each column.

Words that have 2 letters	Words that have 3 letters

Spelling Words

- if
- is
- him
- rip
- fit
- pin

Name ______________________________

Nouns for Places

Listen to the nouns in the Word Bank. Read along. Write nouns from the box to name the places in the pictures.

Word Bank

pool city beach park

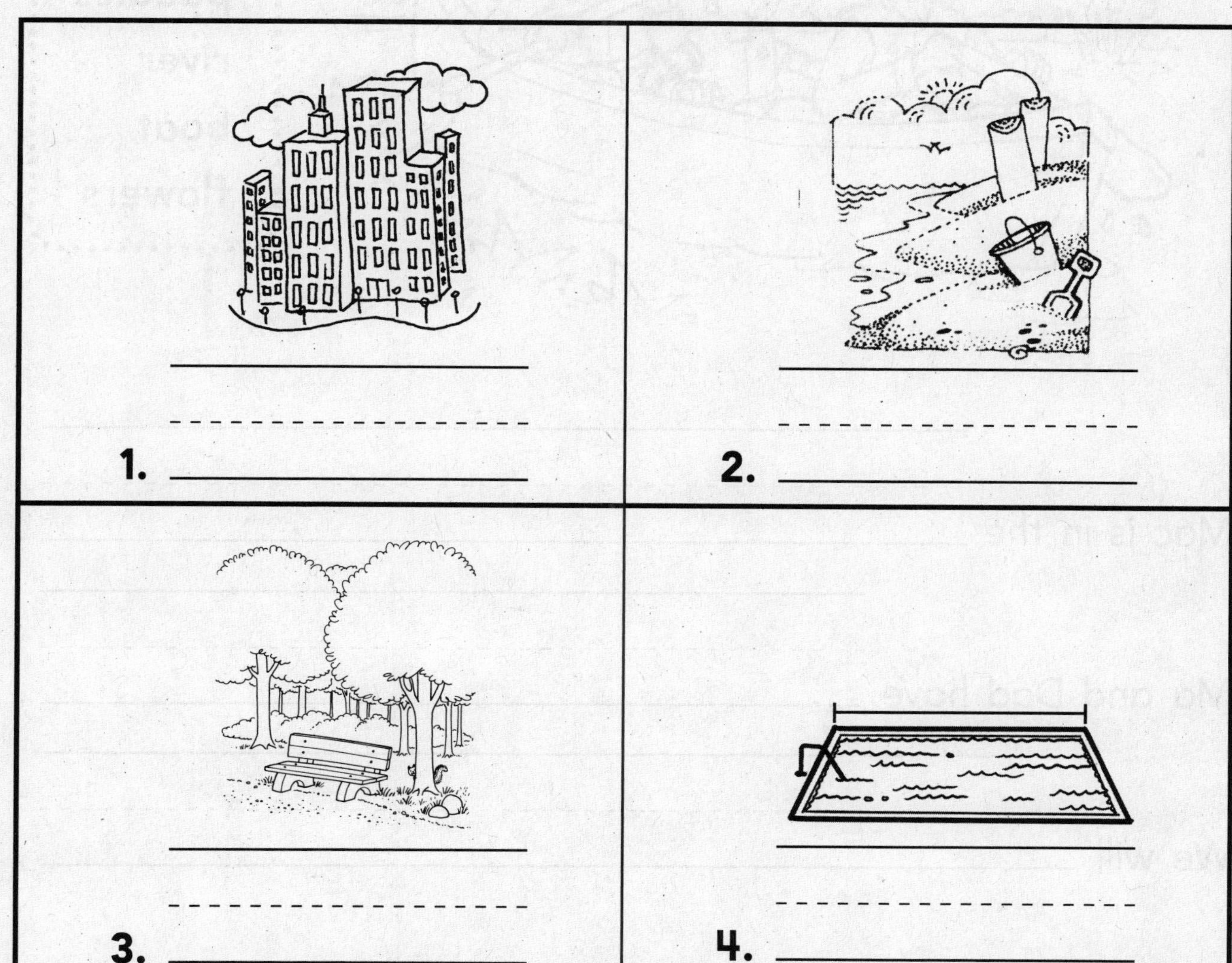

1. ______________

2. ______________

3. ______________

4. ______________

Name ____________________

Details

Listen to the words in the Word Bank. Read along. Fill in each line to write captions for the picture. Choose words from the Word Bank or use your own.

Word Bank

- vests
- paddles
- river
- boat
- flowers

Mac is in the ____________________.

Ma and Dad have ____________________.

We will ____________________.

Name ______________________________

Consonants *b, g*

Name each picture. Think of the ending sound. Write b or g.

1. 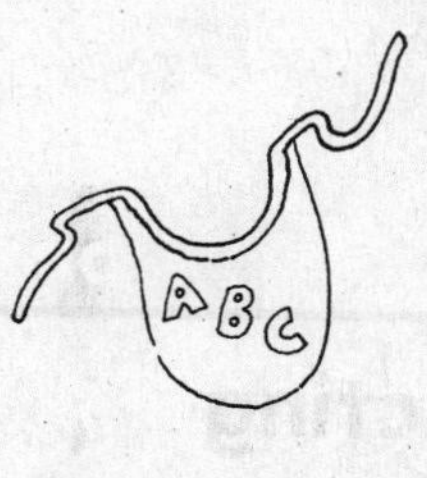

2. 

3. 

4. 

5. 

6. 

Name ____

Understanding Characters

Write or draw things Pop said in the story in the **Speaking** box. Write or draw things Pop did in the **Acting** box.

Speaking	Acting

Name ______________________________

Spelling Words with the Short *i* Sound

Spelling Words

- if
- is
- him
- rip
- fit
- pin

Write the missing letter to complete each Spelling Word. Then write the word.

1. f ___ t ______________
2. p ___ n ______________
3. r ___ p ______________
4. ___ f ______________
5. h ___ m ______________
6. ___ s ______________

Name ______________________________

Words That Name Things

Listen to the nouns in the Word Bank. Read along. Write a noun from the box to name each thing.

Word Bank

- lamp
- milk
- door
- chair
- book

1. ______________________

2. ______________________

3. ______________________

4. ______________________

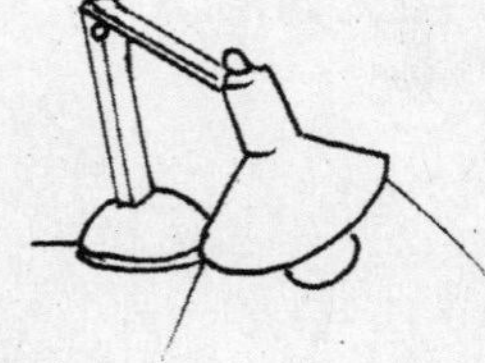

5. ______________________

Name ____________________

Planning My Caption

Draw a picture of your family in a favorite place.

My Family

Write captions that tell about your picture.

Name ________________________________

Spelling Words with the Short *i* Sound

Write the correct word to complete each sentence.

1. We play with ____________. (is, him)

2. What did you ____________? (rip, if)

3. Kip ____________ a pal. (is, him)

4. Do you have a ____________? (pin, him)

5. Can the hat ____________? (pin, fit)

6. Will you play ____________ I do? (fit, if)

Name ___________________________________

Spiral Review

Draw a line under each complete sentence.

1. How will Tim be?
How Tim

2. sits with him
Pop sits with him.

3. Tim takes a sip.
a sip

4. sat at the bed
Rip sat at the bed.

5. Rip and Tim like to play.
Rip and Tim

Name ______________________

Grammar in Writing

Words that name places and things are called **nouns**. Use nouns to name places and things when you write.

The sky is cloudy. The rain falls down.

Listen to the nouns in the Word Bank. Read along. Write nouns from the box to finish the sentences.

Word Bank

- door
- house
- dog
- milk

1. Tim will go in to the ______________ .

2. Do you see the ______________ mat?

3. He has a bit of ______________ .

4. Now he will play with the ______________ .

Name ______________________________

Words to Know

Complete the sentences. Write a word from the box on each line.

Words to Know

do find funny sing no they

1. Look at the ______________ cat!

2. ______________ like to help.

3. What will he ______________ now?

4. Dan will ______________ now.

5. ______________, he did not see the cat.

6. We can ______________ a mat for you.

Name ______________________________

Words with Short *o*

Name each picture. Color the pictures with short o.

Name ______________________________

Consonants *l*, *x*

Finish the rhymes. Write one of the words from the box on the line.

six box

Look at the fox.

It is on the ______.

lot log

Bob did not jog.

Bob sat on a ______.

Name ________________________

Spelling Words with the Short *o* Sound

Sort the words. Write the correct Spelling Words in each column.

Words that rhyme	Words that do not rhyme

Spelling Words

log
dot
top
hot
lot
ox

Name ________________________________

Action Verbs

Listen to the verbs in the Word Bank. Read along. Write verbs from the box to tell about the actions in the pictures.

eat
run
drink
draw

1. ________________________________

2. ________________________________

3. ________________________________

4. ________________________________

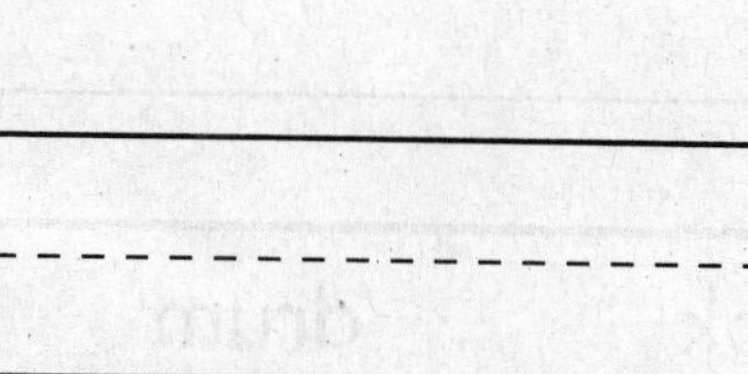

Name ______________________

Using Exact Nouns

Draw two people at school. Show each one doing something different.

Listen to the words in the box. Read along. Write two sentences about your pictures. Tell what each person is doing.

Who	Action Verb	Exact Noun

Who	Action Verb	Exact Noun

ball	book	drum	fish	games
paper	piano	picture	song	teacher

Name ___

Curious George at School
Phonics: Inflection *-s*

Words with Inflection *-s*

Name each picture. Write the word. Use words in the box.

sits	digs	pats	sips	bats	mops

1.

2.

3.

4.

5.

6.

Name ______________________________

Sequence of Events

Write in the chart the events that happen in the story. Tell what happens first, next, and last.

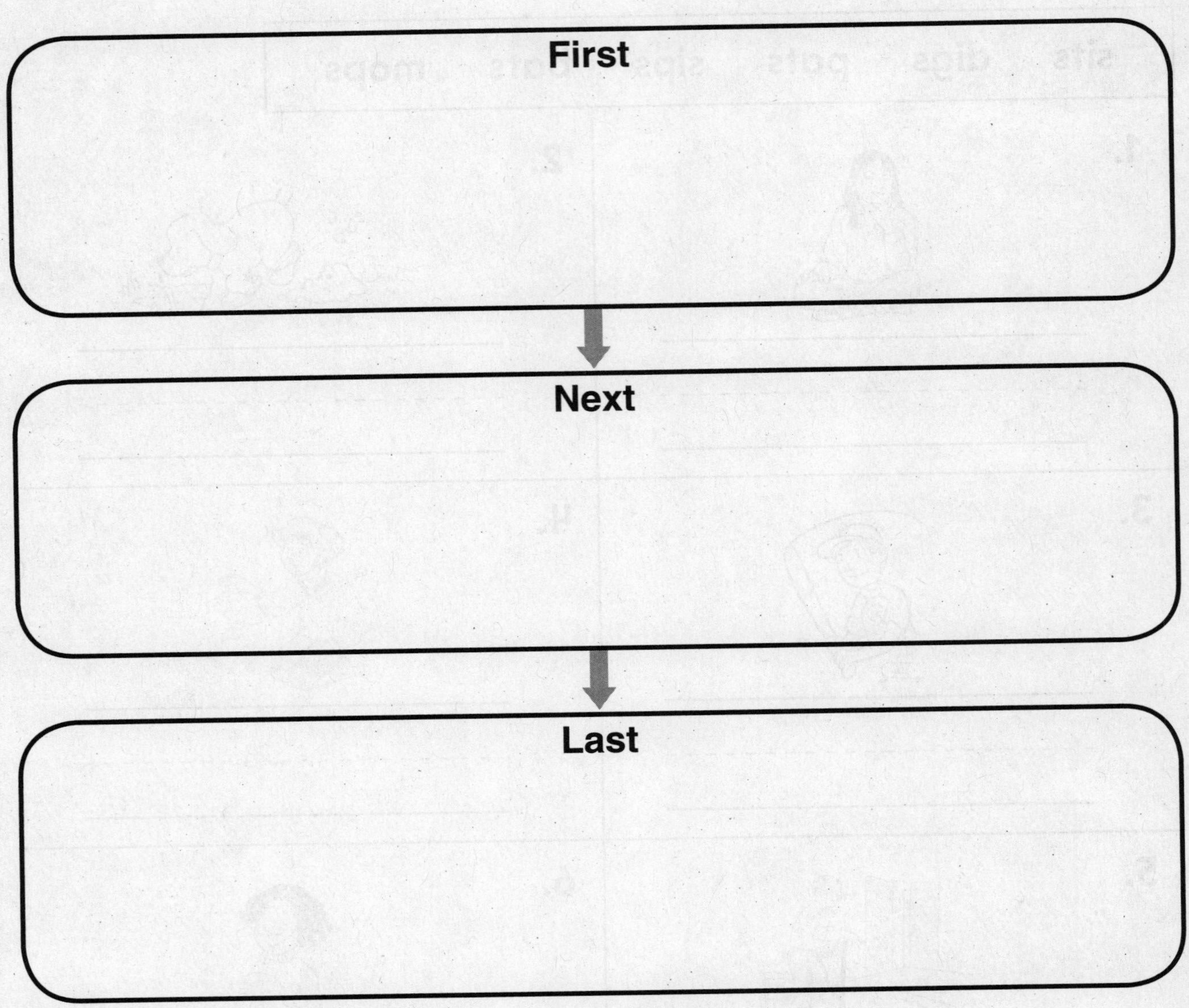

Name ____________________

Spelling Words with the Short *o* Sound

Spelling Words

log
dot
hot
top
lot
ox

Write the missing letter to complete each Spelling Word. Then write the word.

1. l ____ t ____________________
2. l ____ g ____________________
3. h ____ t ____________________
4. ____ x ____________________
5. t ____ p ____________________
6. d ____ t ____________________

Name ______________________

More Words That Show Action

Listen to the verbs in the Word Bank. Read along. Write a verb from the box to name each action in the picture.

Word Bank

- climb
- slide
- jump
- swing
- throw

Name ______________________________

Planning My Sentences

Write an action verb at the top of each box. Draw a picture to go with the verb.

Name ________________________________

Spelling Words with the Short *o* Sound

Write the correct word to complete each sentence.

1. A ______________ is not big. (hot, dot)

2. The ______________ is big. (log, hot)

3. We have a ______________ of cats. (lot, top)

4. Pam is at the ______________ . (dog, top)

5. Do you have a ______________ pot? (hot, log)

6. Did you ever see an ______________ ? (ox, hot)

Spiral Review

Draw a line under each correct statement.

1. We get the box.
   we get the box.

2. Bob can help
   Bob can help.

3. He will mix it.
   he will mix it.

4. We have fun.
   we have fun

5. We like to sing
   We like to sing.

Name ______________________

Grammar in Writing

Words that tell what people and animals do are called **verbs**.

They run on the playground.

Circle the verb to finish each sentence. Write the verb on the line.

1. Sal can ______________ with a bat.

hit **fit**

2. They ______________ big bags.

make **sit**

3. We ______________ the dogs.

go **see**

4. Bob and Meg ______________ a cat.

find **hop**

Name ______________________________

Words to Know

Complete the sentences. Write a word from the box on each line.

Words to Know

all	does	here	me	my	who

1. Lin is ______________ pal.
2. Sam will come ______________ to play.
3. He likes to play with ______________ .
4. I will see ______________ is there.
5. Sam ______________ a funny trick.
6. We will take up ______________ the mats.

Name ______________________________

Words with Short *e*

Circle the word that matches each picture.

1.

win web

2.

mat men

3.

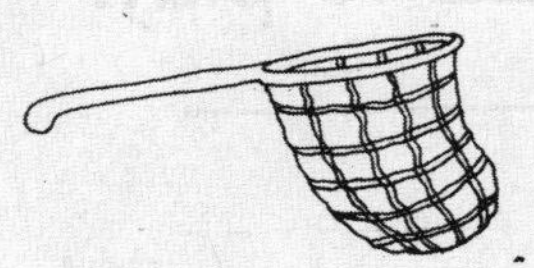

net can

4.

pen pin

5.

ten tin

6.

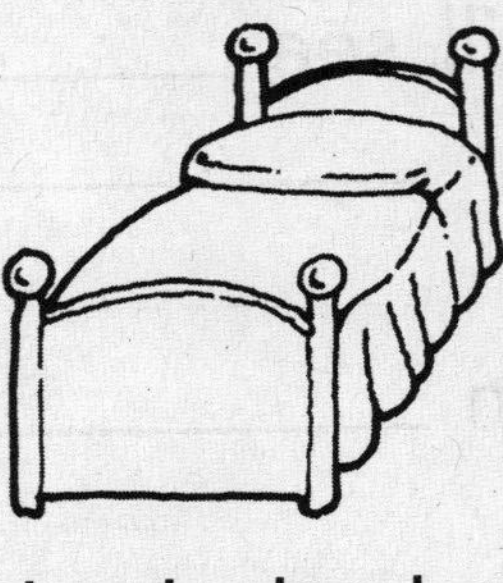

bad bed

Name ______________________________

Consonants *y, w*

Name each picture. Think of the beginning sound. Write y or w.

1.

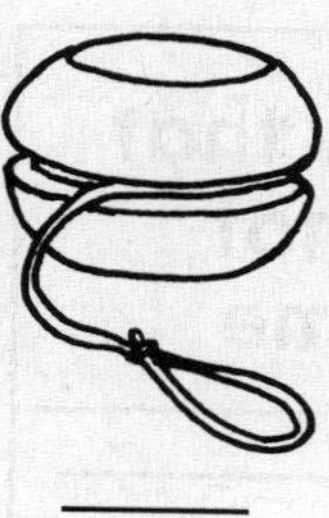

____

2.

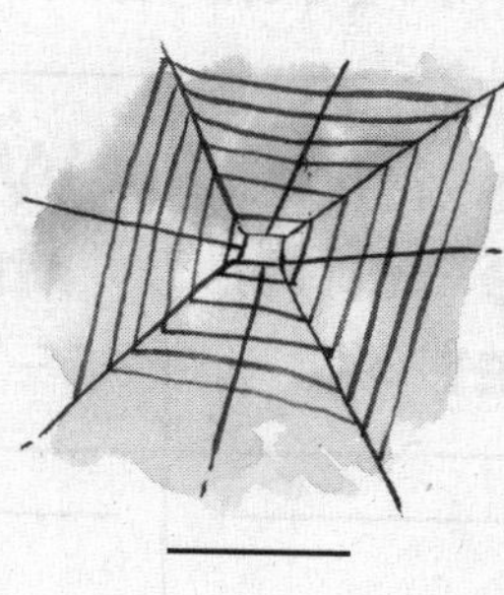

____

3.

____

4.

____

5.

____

6.

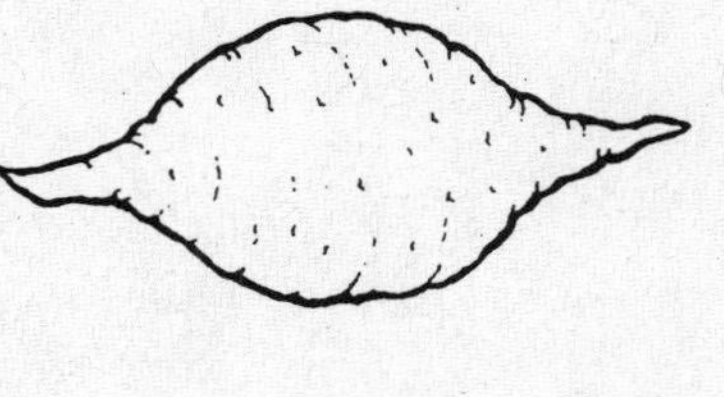

____

Name ____________________

Spelling Words with the Short *e* Sound

Sort the words. Write the correct Spelling Words in each column.

Words that rhyme with get	Words that rhyme with den	Words that do not rhyme

Spelling Words

yet
web
pen
wet
leg
hen

Name ______________________________

Adjectives for Size

Listen to the adjectives. Read along. Circle the adjective that describes what the picture shows. Write the adjective.

1. small ______________ big ______________

2. long ______________ short ______________

3. narrow ______________ wide ______________

4. short ______________ tall ______________

Name ______

Using Words That Are Just Right

Cross out the word that is the same in each sentence. Listen to the words in the box. Read along. Write a better word from the box.

Word Bank

busy	large	new	sweet
round	kind	square	tall

1. Our town has a good market. ______

2. Mom and I get good apples there. ______

3. We got a good cake for Dad. ______

4. The man that helps us is good. ______

Name ______________________________

Lucia's Neighborhood
Phonics: Consonants *k, v, j*

Consonants *k, v, j*

Name each picture. Think of the beginning sound. Write k, v, or j.

1. 

2. 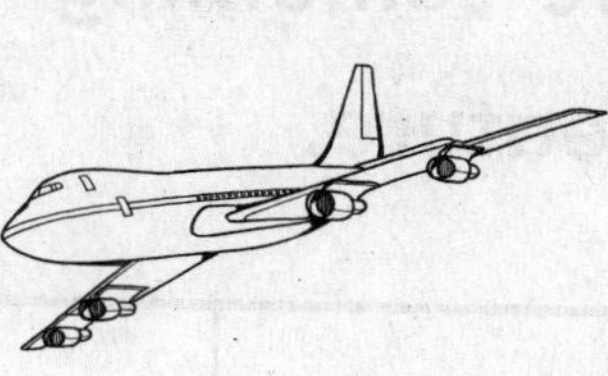

3. 

4. 

5. 

6. 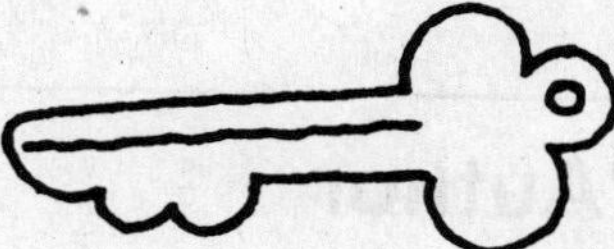

7. 

8. 

9. 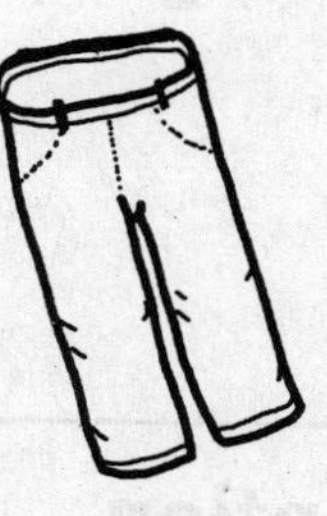

Name ______________________________

Text and Graphic Features

Listen to the name of each feature and read along. Write something to tell the purpose of the feature.

Feature	Purpose
Title	
Author	
Photograph	
Caption	

Name ______________________________

Spelling Words with the Short *e* Sound

Write the missing letter to complete each Spelling Word. Then write the word.

1. y ___ t ______________
2. h ___ n ______________
3. w ___ b ______________
4. l ___ g ______________
5. p ___ n ______________
6. w ___ t ______________

Spelling Words

yet
web
pen
wet
leg
hen

Name ______________________________

Adjectives for Shape

Listen to and follow the directions.

1. Circle the shape that is **round**.

2. Circle the shape that is **flat**.

3. Circle the shape that is **square**.

4. Circle the shape that is **curved**.

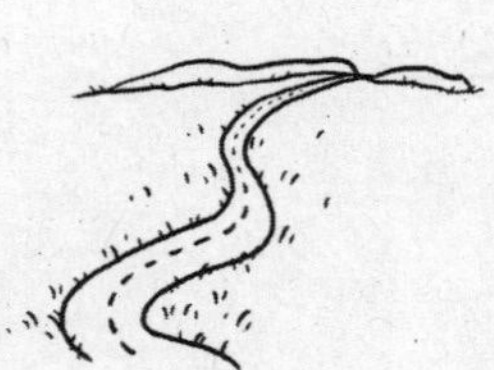

Name ______________________________

Spelling Words with the Short *e* Sound

Write the correct word to complete each sentence.

1. He is not here ______________. (yet, web)

2. The ______________ is big. (wet, hen)

3. My ______________ is red. (pen, wet)

4. The dog is all ______________. (wet, hen)

5. I can hop on my ______________. (yet, leg)

6. I can see a ______________. (wet, web)

Name ______________________________

Spiral Review

Circle the end mark in each sentence. Then circle statement or question.

1. What can you find? — statement / question

2. I can find a fan. — statement / question

3. What will you do now? — statement / question

4. I will sing. — statement / question

5. Do you have a pet? — statement / question

6. Yes, I have a pet dog. — statement / question

Name ______________________________

Grammar in Writing

Words that describe people, animals, or things are called **adjectives**. Adjectives can describe size or shape.

The house is big. (size)
The truck is wide. (shape)

Listen to the adjectives in the Word Banks. Read along. Write on the line an adjective for size.

Word Bank
long
little

1. A leg is ______________ .

2. A dot is ______________ .

Write on the line an adjective for shape.

Word Bank
flat
round

3. A map is ______________ .

4. A log is ______________ .

Name ______________________

Words to Know

Draw a line to the word that completes the sentence. Write the word on the line.

1. Tom will ______________ the sled. **hold**

2. It was ______________ to sit for a bit. **full**

3. All the bags are ______________ . **pull**

4. Mel has ______________ pals. **friend**

5. Cam is my ______________ . **good**

6. Mom will ______________ my books for me. **many**

Name ______________________________

Gus Takes the Train
Phonics: Short *u*

Words with Short *u*

Write the missing letter. Read the word.

1.

p ___ p

2.

c ___ p

3.

m ___ d

4.

t ___ b

5.

f ___ n

6.

___ p

Name ______________________________

Gus Takes the Train
Phonics: Short *u*

More Words With Short *u*

Write the missing letter. Read the word.

1.

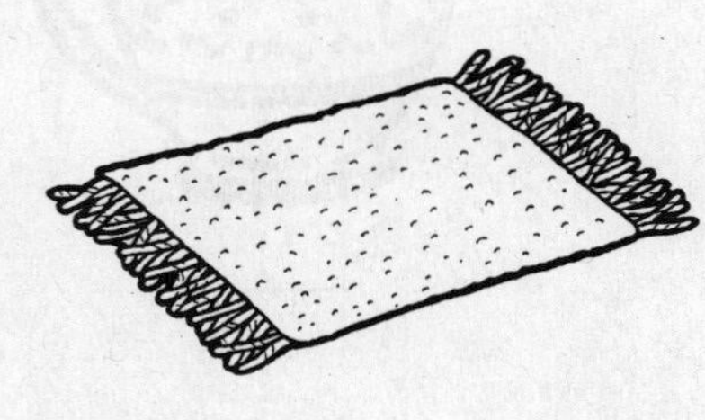

___ u g

2.

___ u n

3.

___ u s

4.

___ u t

5.

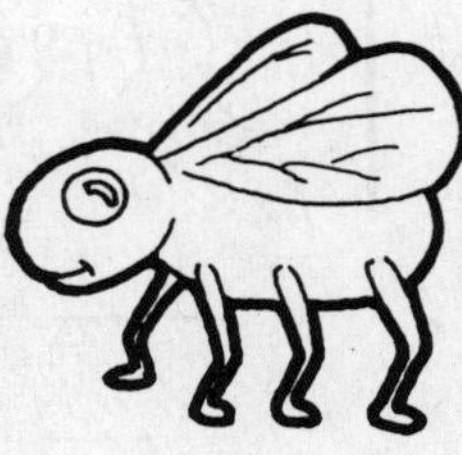

___ u g

6.

___ u n

Name ______________________

Spelling Words with the Short *u* Sound

Sort the words. Write the correct Spelling Words in each column.

Words that rhyme	Words that do not rhyme

Spelling Words

up
bug
mud
nut
hug
tub

Name ______________________________

Adjectives for Color

Listen to the directions. Read along. Color each picture.

1. Color the cap **blue**.

2. Color the toy **yellow**.

3. Color the ball **orange**.

4. Color the apple **red**.

5. Color the bug **black**.

Name ______________________________

Telling More

Complete each sentence. Choose an adjective from the box to tell more.

big	many	ten	mad
bad	good	red	tan
sad	funny	hot	wet

1. Dad and I get on a bus.

   Dad and I get on a ______________ bus.

2. We go to a park.

   We go to a ______________ park.

3. We see a man with pets.

   We see a man with ______________ pets.

4. Dad gets me a hat!

   Dad gets me a ______________ hat!

Name ______________________

Consonants *qu, z*

Name each picture. Think of the beginning sound. Write qu or z.

1.

2.

3.

4.

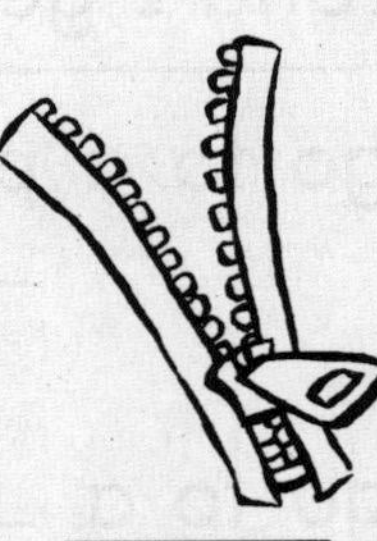

5.

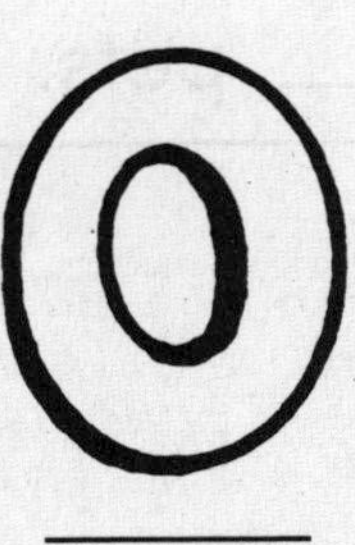

6.

Name ________________________________

Gus Takes the Train
Comprehension: Story Structure

Story Structure

Write or draw pictures to show the characters, setting, and plot of the story.

Characters	Setting
Plot	
Beginning	
Middle	
End	

Name ______________________

Spelling Words with the Short *u* Sound

Spelling Words

up
bug
mud
nut
hug
tub

Write the missing letter to complete each Spelling Word. Then write the word.

1. n ____ t ______________
2. b ____ g ______________
3. m ____ d ______________
4. ____ p ______________
5. t ____ b ______________
6. h ____ g ______________

Name ______________________________

Adjectives for Number

Listen to the adjectives in the Word Bank. Read along. Write a word from the box to describe each picture.

Word Bank

two three four six

1.

____

2.

____

3.

____

4.

____

Name ______________________

Spelling Words with the Short *u* Sound

Write the correct word to complete each sentence.

1. Dad likes to ______________ the cat. (up, hug)

2. A ______________ is on my leg! (bug, hug)

3. Put the mat ______________ on top. (nut, up)

4. I got wet in the ______________. (tub, bug)

5. Do you have a ______________ for me? (nut, mud)

6. The pig likes to play in the ______________. (mud, hug)

Name ____________________

Spiral Review

Circle the pronoun that can take the place of the underlined word or words. Then write the pronoun.

1. The box is full.

____________ is full.

It **They**

2. Peg and Ned play.

____________ play.

She **They**

3. Ted helps.

____________ helps.

He **It**

4. Nan has fun.

____________ has fun.

They **She**

Name ______________________________

Grammar in Writing

Words that describe people, places, animals, or things are called **adjectives**. Adjectives can describe color and number.

The train is black. The five seats are red.

Finish each sentence with an adjective for number. Use the Word Bank.

Word Bank
one
three

1. I see ____________ flowers.

2. I see ____________ cat.

Listen to and follow the directions.

3. Draw **two** apples.
Color the apples **red**.

4. Draw **four** bugs.
Color the bugs **black**.

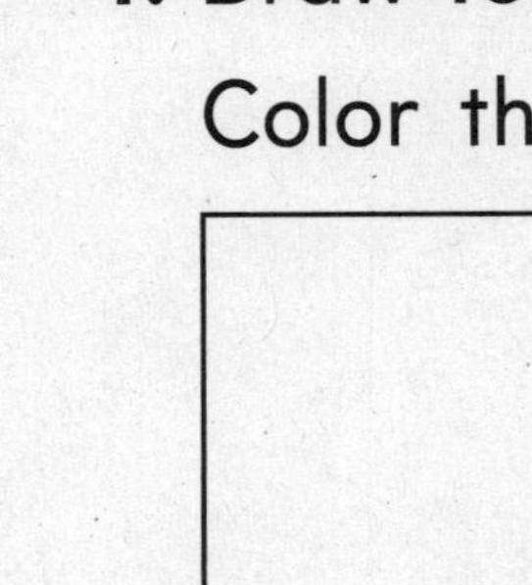

Name ______________________

Words to Know

Fill in the blanks to complete the sentences. Write a word from the box on each line.

Words to Know

hear	call	come
said	every	away

1. Does ______________ dog like to play?

2. Mem ______________ she did not see the dog.

3. Jack will ______________ to help me.

4. Sam and Jill are far ______________ .

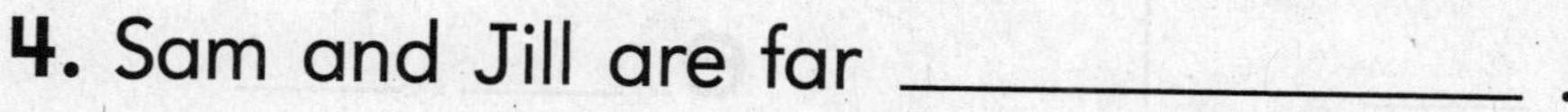

5. Did you ______________ the clock tick?

6. Von will ______________ on me to sing.

Name ______________________________

Jack and the Wolf
Phonics: Double Final Consonants and *ck*

Double Final Consonants and *ck*

Name each picture. Write the letters from the box that stand for the ending sound.

ck	gg	ll	ss

1. q u a ___ ___

2. h i ___ ___

3. l o ___ ___

4. e ___ ___

5. 

d o ___ ___

6. 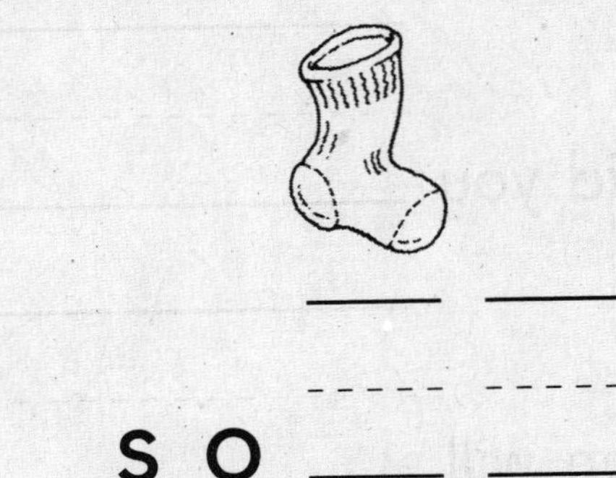

s o ___ ___

Name ______________________________

Jack and the Wolf
Phonics: Double Final Consonants and *ck*

Double Final Consonants and *ck*

Circle the letters to make the word that matches the picture. Write the letters.

1\. 

b u ___ ___

ck zz

2\. 

t a ___ ___

ss ck

3\. 

p u ___ ___

gg ff

4\. 

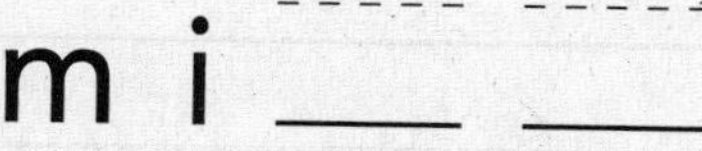

m i ___ ___

ss tt

5\. 

h i ___ ___

ss ll

6\. 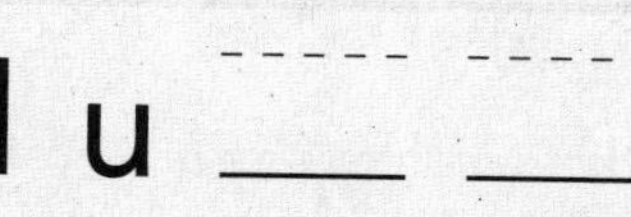

d u ___ ___

ll ck

Name ______________________________

Spelling Words with the Short *a* Sound

Sort the words. Write the correct Spelling Words in each column.

Words that begin with a vowel	Words that begin with a consonant

Spelling Words

an
bad
can
had
cat
ran

Name ______________________________

What Is a Sentence?

Draw a line under each sentence.

1. The friends play.

2. a cat

3. The dog runs.

4. sit

Draw lines to make sentences.

5. The hen	sits on a rock.
6. Gram	like to sing.
7. Jack	sits on eggs.
8. We	makes a doll.

Name ______________________________

Using Sense Words

deep
hot
loud
small
soft
sunny
sweet
warm

Listen to the sense words in the box and the sentences below. Read along. Write words from the box to finish the sentences about the picture.

1. The bananas smell ____________.

2. The lion's fur feels ____________.

3. The seal's bark sounds ____________.

4. The monkeys look ____________.

Name ______________________

Short *a*, Double Final Consonants, and *ck*

Name each picture. Write words from the box.

fill	wag	yam	quick	van	neck

1. ______________________

2. ______________________

3. ______________________

4. ______________________

5. ______________________

6. ______________________

Name ______________________________

Understanding Characters

Use the chart to tell what Jack and his friends think and do.

Thinking	Acting

Name ______________________________

Spelling Words with the Short *a* Sound

Spelling Words

- an
- bad
- can
- had
- cat
- ran

Write the Spelling Words that rhyme with man.

1. ______________

2. ______________

3. ______________

Write the Spelling Words that rhyme with dad.

4. ______________ 5. ______________

Write the Spelling Word that rhymes with sat.

6. ______________

Name ______________________________

Is It a Sentence?

Draw a line under each sentence.

1. The dog naps.
   naps

2. Tim and Jim
   Tim and Jim run away.

3. the friends
   The friends come to help.

4. The man sits down.
   sits

5. sings
   He sings.

6. get up
   The dog will get up.

Name ______________________

Jack and the Wolf
Writing: Write to Describe

Planning My Sentences

Listen to the labels in the web and read along. Write and draw details that describe your topic. You do not have to write words for every sense.

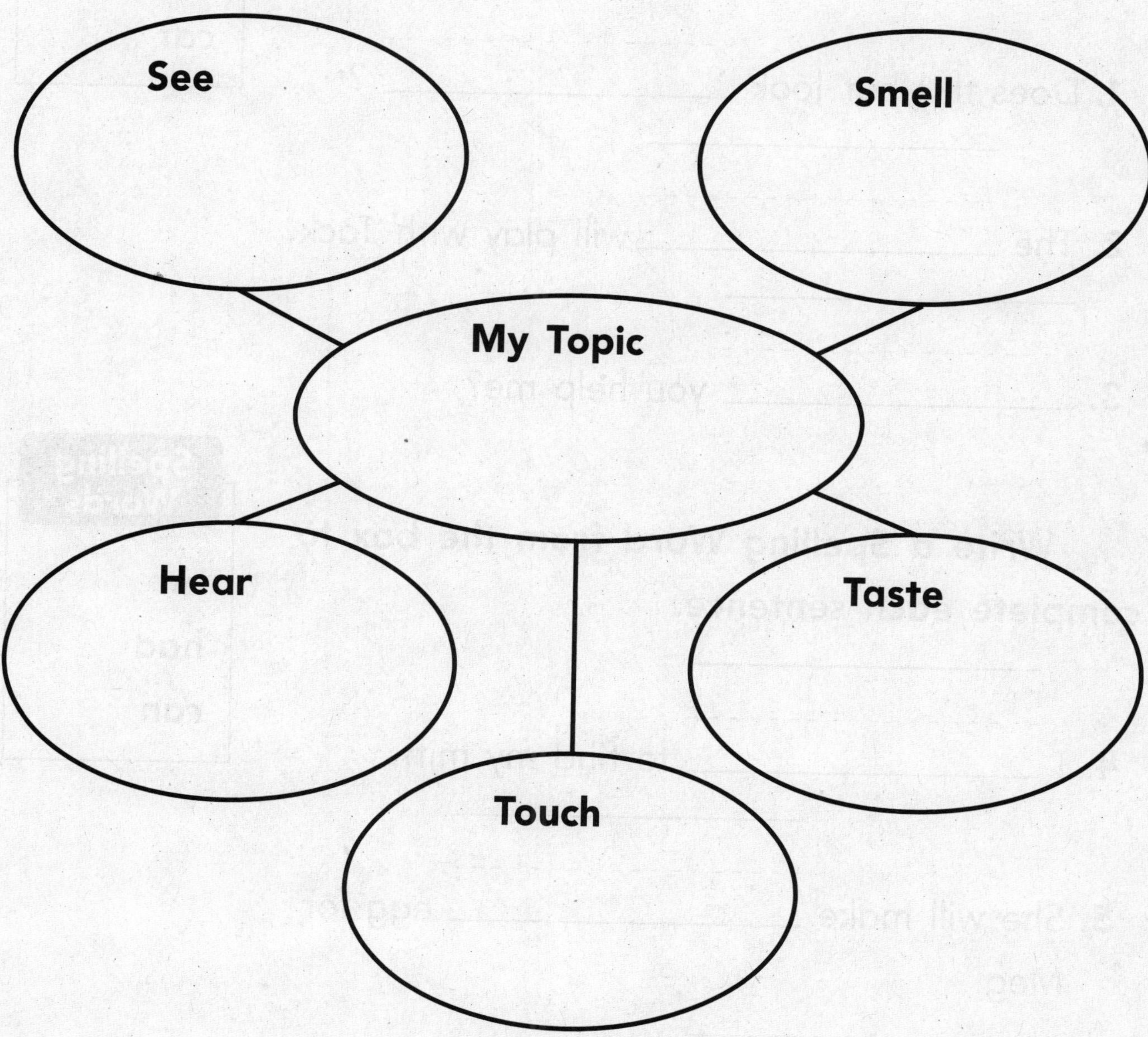

Name ____________________

Spelling Words with the Short *a* Sound

Write a Spelling Word from the box to complete each sentence.

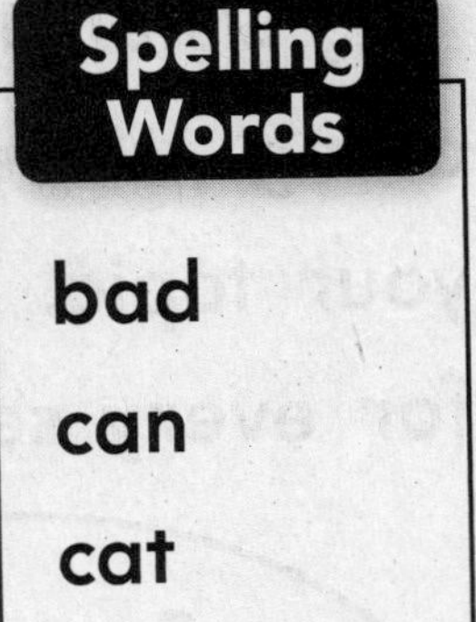

Spelling Words

bad
can
cat

1. Does this hat look ____________ ?

2. The ____________ will play with Jack.

3. ____________ you help me?

Write a Spelling Word from the box to complete each sentence.

Spelling Words

an
had
ran

4. I ____________ to find my mitt.

5. She will make ____________ egg for Meg.

6. I ____________ out to play.

Name ______________________________

Spiral Review

Listen to the nouns in the Word Bank. Read along. Write a noun from the box to name each picture.

Word Bank

- girl
- pig
- horse
- baby

1. ______________________

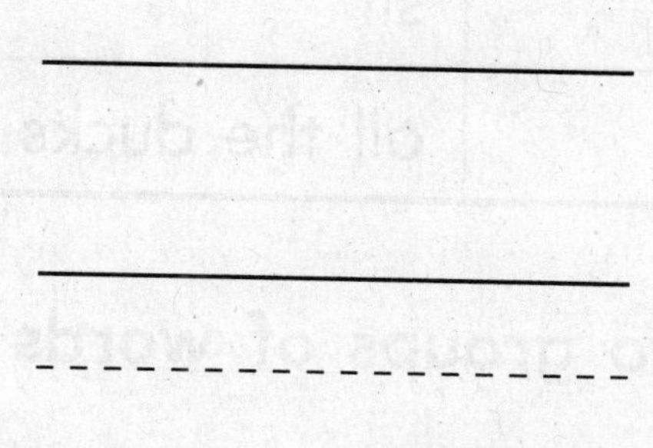

2. ______________________

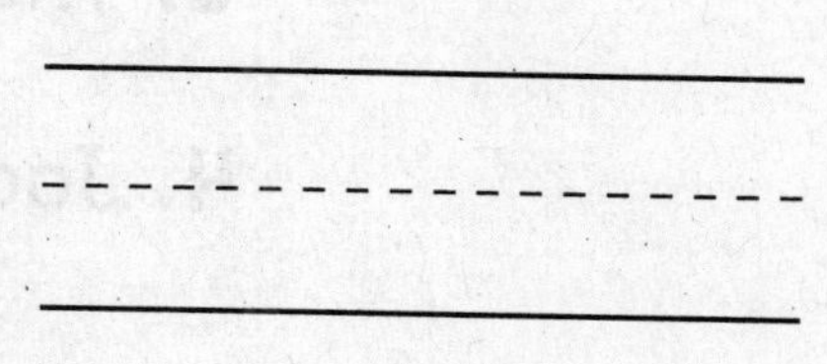

3. ______________________

4. ______________________

Name ______________________________

Grammar in Writing

A sentence is a group of words. A sentence tells who or what. It also tells what someone or something does or did.

Sentence	Not a Sentence
All the ducks sit.	sit
	all the ducks

Circle the two groups of words that are not sentences.

1. We have fun.

2. get mad

3. The dog runs away.

4. Jack

Add words to make the word groups you circled into complete sentences. Write the new sentences.

5. ______________________________

6. ______________________________

Name ______________________________

Words to Know

Fill in the blanks to complete the sentences.

Words to Know

animal	why	how
some	make	of

1. Tell me ______________ you like to sing.

2. The bug can ______________ a hut out of mud!

3. Bob will go with ______________ friends.

4. He can tell you ______________ to bat.

5. Six ______________ the bags are full.

6. What ______________ do you have as a pet?

Name ______________________

Clusters with *r*

Name each picture. Write letters from the box to complete the word.

br	cr	dr	gr	tr

1. 

___ ___ i n

2. 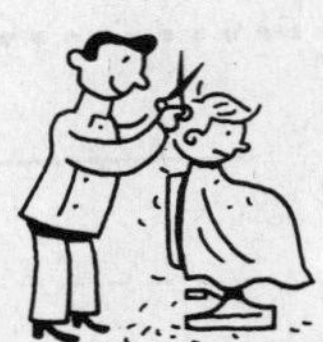

___ ___ i m

3. 

___ ___ i p

4. 

___ ___ i b

5. 

___ ___ i p

6. 

___ ___ i m

Name ____________________

Clusters with *r*

Name each picture. Circle the letters that stand for the beginning sounds. Write the letters to make the word.

1.

fr cr

___ ___

___ ___ a b

2.

pr tr

___ ___

___ ___ a p

3.

pr fr

___ ___

___ ___ o g

4.

gr pr

___ ___

___ ___ i l l

5.

dr gr

___ ___

___ ___ u m

6.

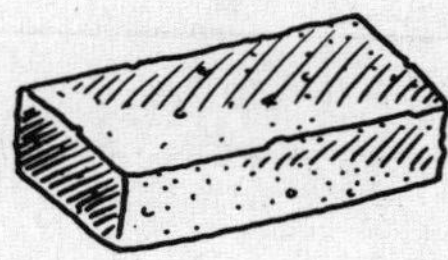

gr br

___ ___

___ ___ i c k

Name ______

Spelling Words with the Short *i* Sound

Sort the words. Write the correct Spelling Words in each column.

Words that begin with a vowel	Words that begin with a consonant

Spelling Words

in
will
did
sit
six
big

Name ____________________

The Naming Part

Circle the subject, or naming part, in each sentence.

1. Dogs run.

2. The ants make a nest.

3. The cat comes to me.

4. The ducks peck.

5. A bull kicks.

6. The bug makes a web.

7. The pigs play in the mud.

8. A fox sits on a log.

Name ______________________

Adjectives

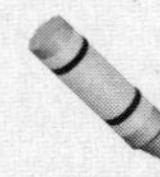 Draw a picture of an animal doing something.

Word Bank

big
small
slow
loud
quiet
soft
young

Listen to the adjectives in the Word Bank. Read along. Complete each sentence with a word from the Word Bank or your own adjective.

1. The animal is ______________.
2. The animal is ______________.
3. The animal is ______________.
4. The animal is ______________.

Name ______________________

Short *i* and Clusters with *r*

Write words that rhyme. Use the words in the box.

trick	grab	dress	drill	grass	quit	tracks	truck

1. brick ____________

2. grill ____________

3. press ____________

4. crab ____________

5. cracks ____________

6. duck ____________

7. sit ____________

8. brass ____________

Name ______________________________

Details

Use the web map to show the topic, main ideas, and supporting details in **How Animals Communicate.**

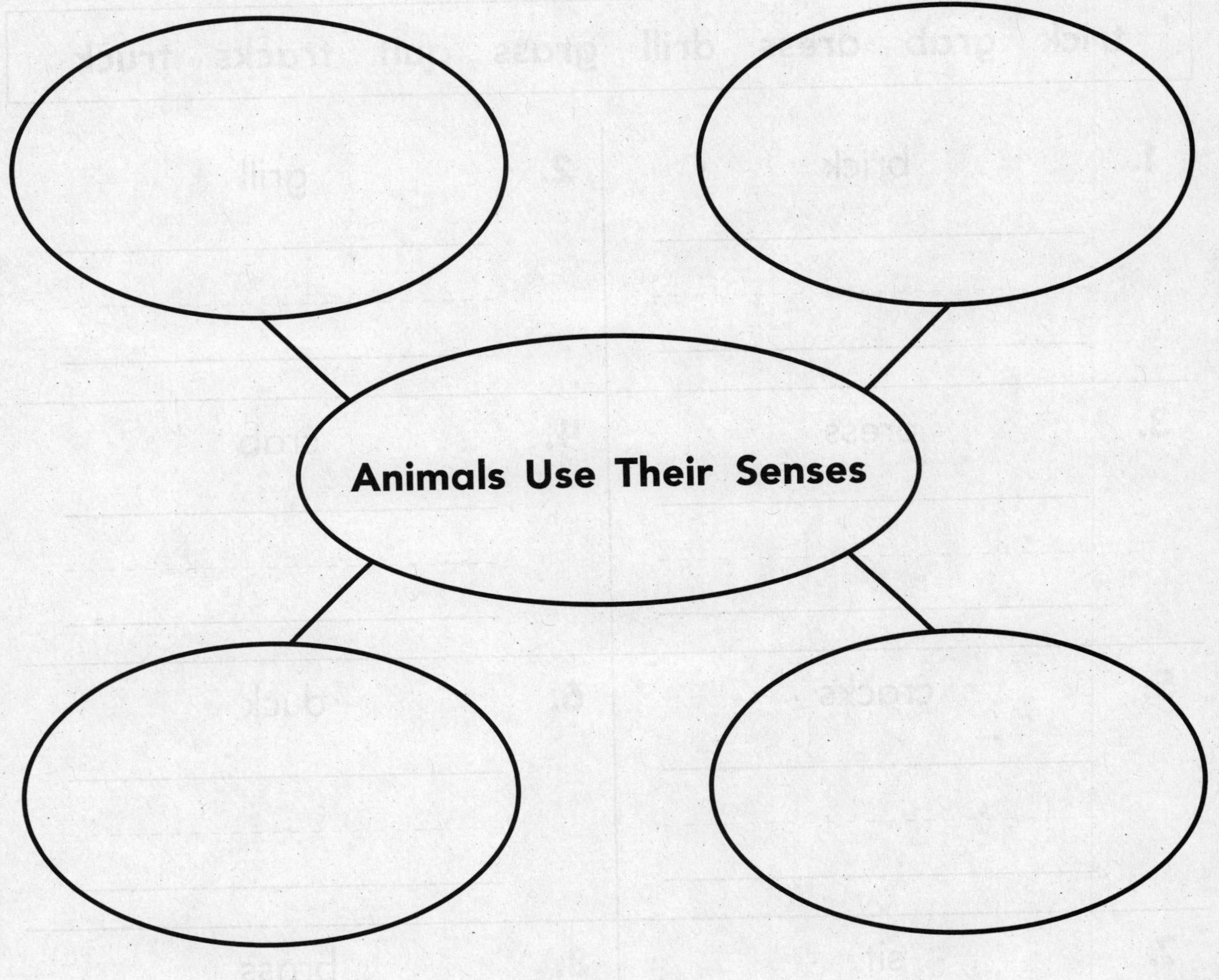

Name ____________________

Spelling Words with the Short *i* Sound

Spelling Words

- in
- will
- did
- sit
- six
- big

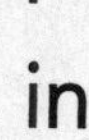 Circle the Spelling Word that names the picture. Then write the word.

1. six
sip

____

2. pin
in

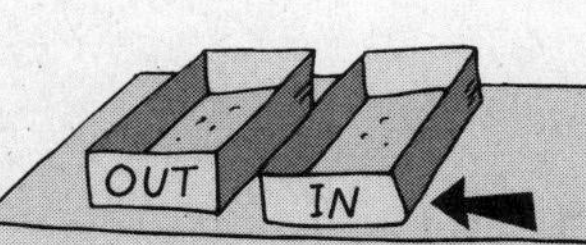

____

3. fit
sit

____

4. big
bag

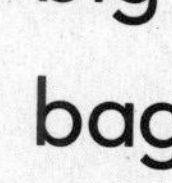

____

Write a Spelling Word that rhymes with each word below.

5. hid ____________________

6. fill ____________________

Name ______________________________

The Action Part

Circle the predicate, or action part, in each sentence.

1. Nick puts on his cap.

2. Ben finds a nut.

3. Jill puts the duck in the tub.

4. The ants make a nest.

5. Hens sit on eggs.

6. Nell helps her mom.

7. The dog plays.

8. The cat naps.

Name ____________________

Planning My Poem

Write and draw details that describe your topic. Listen to the names of the senses and read along. You do not have to write words for every sense.

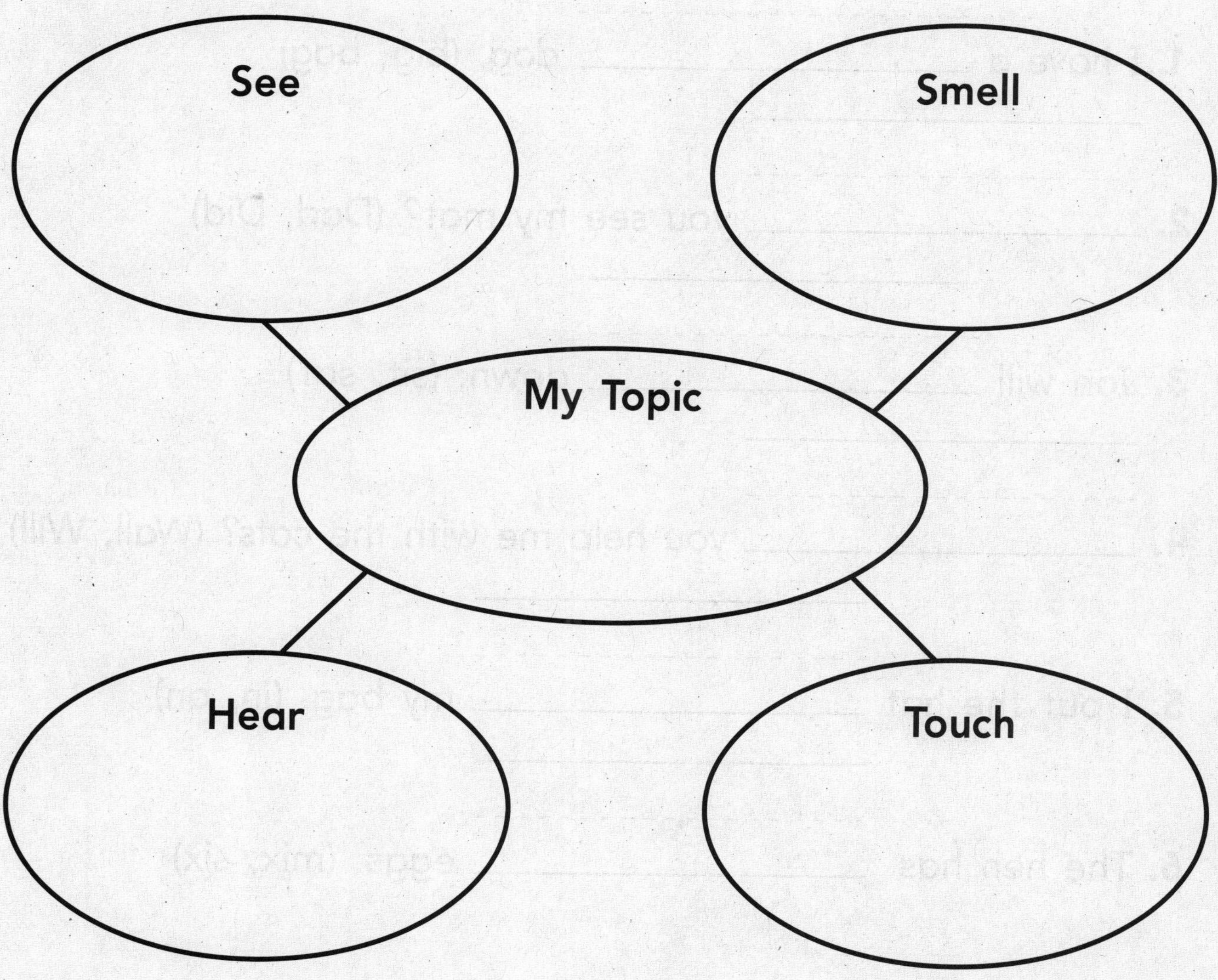

Name ______________________

Spelling Words with the Short *i* Sound

Write the correct word to complete each sentence.

1. I have a ______________ dog. (big, bag)

2. ______________ you see my mat? (Dad, Did)

3. Jon will ______________ down. (sit, sat)

4. ______________ you help me with the cats? (Wall, Will)

5. I put the hat ______________ my bag. (in, an)

6. The hen has ______________ eggs. (mix, six)

Name ______________________

Spiral Review

Listen to the nouns in the Word Bank. Read along. Write a noun from the box to name each picture.

1.  ______________

2. 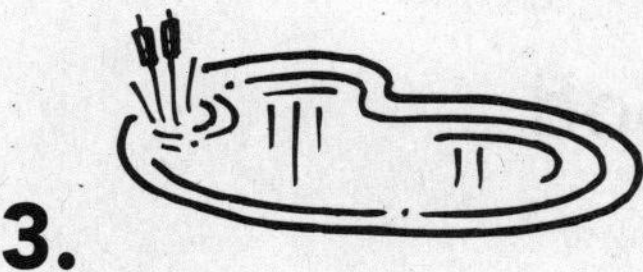 ______________

3.  ______________

4. ______________

Name ______________________

Grammar in Writing

Every sentence has two parts. The naming part is called the **subject**. The action part is called the **predicate**.

Example: The dogs bark loudly.
subject **predicate**

Circle the two groups of words that are not sentences.

1. The fox plays.
2. The kittens
3. A pig sits in the mud.
4. look for food

Add words to make the word groups you circled into complete sentences.

5. ______________________

6. ______________________

Name ____________________

Words to Know

Choose the word that fits best in the sentence. Write the word on the line.

1. Jen will fix (her, she, today) bed. ____________________

2. I (our, here, would) like to help. ____________________

3. (Her, Now, She) is my friend. ____________________

4. We have a lot to do (our, today, she). ____________________

5. We did (she, here, our) job! ____________________

6. We can play (our, now, her). ____________________

Name ______________________________

Clusters with *l*

Name each picture. Write the first two letters to make the word.

1.

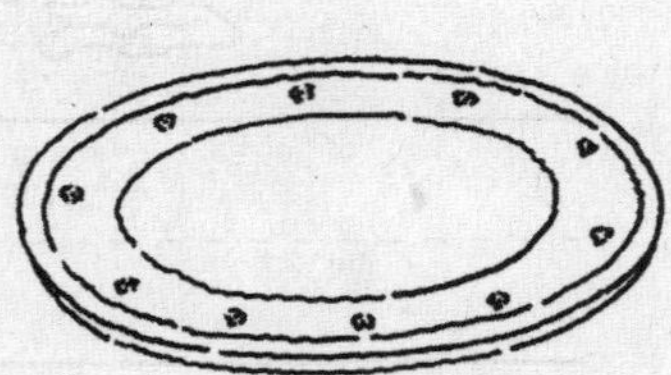

__ __ a t e

2.

__ __ a y

3.

__ __ o c k

4.

__ __ a d

5.

__ __ a t

6.

__ __ e d

Name ____________________

Clusters with *l*

Circle the word to finish the sentence.
Write the word.

1.

She will ____________.

slip slap

2.

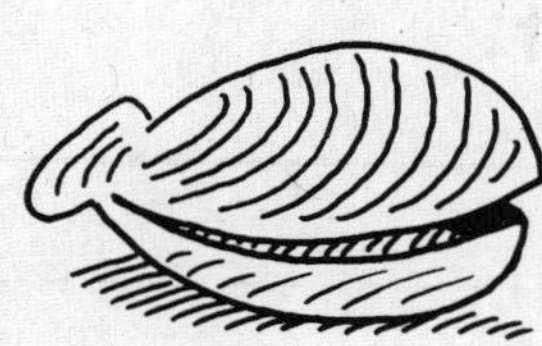

This is a ____________.

clam blot

3.

Who will ____________ this?

slip flip

4.

I have a ____________.

plan blab

5.

This is a big ____________.

blot flap

6.

He is ____________ to play.

clap glad

Name ______________________________

Spelling Words with the Short *o* Sound

Spelling Words

on
fox
got
hop
pop
not

Write the Spelling Words that rhyme with dot.

1. ____________ 2. ____________

Write the Spelling Words that rhyme with top.

3. ____________ 4. ____________

Write the Spelling Word that rhymes with ox.

5. ____________

Write the Spelling Word that rhymes with Don.

6. ____________

What Is a Statement?

Draw a line under each statement.

1. He makes a drum.
2. sings
3. She plays well.
4. Our band will win.
5. Bill and Sam
6. Nick claps for us.

Use a word from the box to make each group of words a statement.

Word Bank

listen
Meg

7. ______________ plays the drums.

8. Ken and Kim ______________ .

Name ______________________

Using Exact Adjectives

Fill in the blanks in the draft of the thank-you note. Listen to the adjectives in the Word Bank. Read along. Choose adjectives from the box. Write your own words, too.

Word Bank

hot	huge	icy	tall	round
soft	striped	sweet	green	yellow

____

Dear ______________________,

Thank you for the ______________________ ______________________ ______________________. It is ______________________ ______________________. I like the ______________________ ______________________ ______________________.

Name ______________________________

Short *i* and Clusters with *l*

A Musical Day
Phonics: Short *i* and Clusters with *l*

Name each picture. Circle the letters that stand for the beginning sounds. Write the word.

1.

cr gr

____

2.

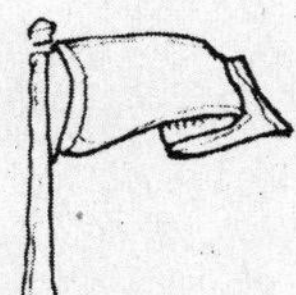

fl fr

____

3.

fl sl

____

4.

br dr

____

5.

gr dr

____

6.

pl bl

____

Name ______________________________

A Musical Day
Comprehension: Sequence of Events

Sequence of Events

Use the chart to tell the sequence of events in the story.

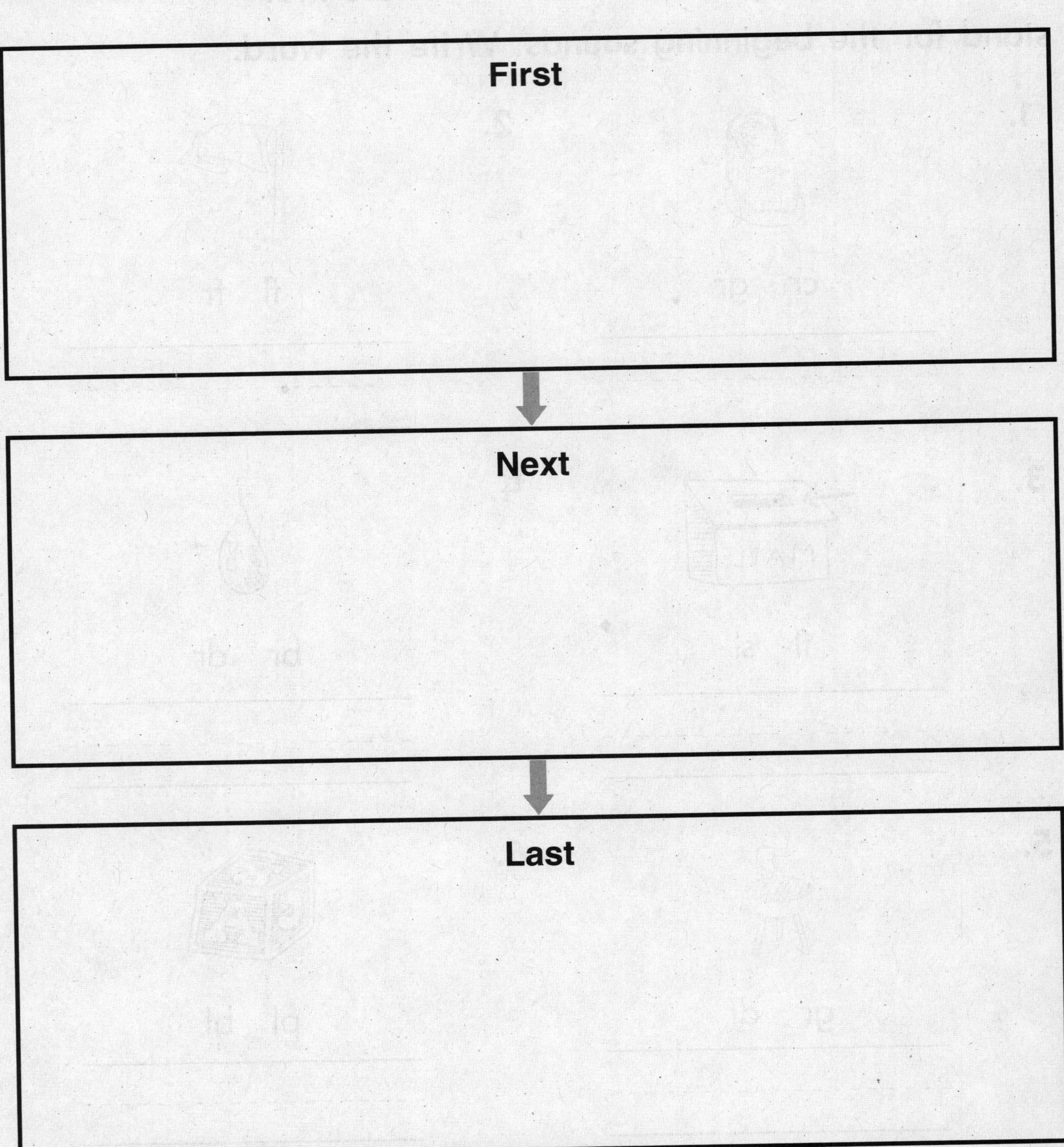

Name ____________________

Spelling Words with the Short *o* Sound

Write the missing letter to complete each Spelling Word. Then write the word.

1. f ____ x ____________________

2. n ____ t ____________________

3. p ____ p ____________________

4. h ____ p ____________________

5. ____ n ____________________

6. g ____ t ____________________

Spelling Words

on
got
fox
hop
pop
not

Name ______________________________

A Musical Day
Grammar: Statements

Writing Statements

Circle the capital letter that begins each statement and the period that ends it.

1. Clem likes my song.
2. She sings for her mom.
3. Her mom sings, too.
4. They like to sing.

Write each statement correctly.

5. tess has a drum set

____

6. she plays it a lot

____

Name ______________________________

Planning My Thank-You Note

I will write my thank-you note to

______________________________.

Draw a picture of what you are thankful for. Write some details for your note.

I am thankful for

Name ______________________

Spelling Words with the Short *o* Sound

Spelling Words

on
fox
got
pop
not
hop

Write a Spelling Word to complete each sentence.

1. This animal is a ______________ .

2. I ______________ a dog from Bob.

3. I like caps but ______________ hats.

4. The bag will ______________ if you fill it up.

5. The fox will ______________ off the box.

6. Do not sit ______________ the bed.

Name ______________________

Spiral Review

Listen to the verbs in the Word Bank. Read along. Write a verb from the box to name each action.

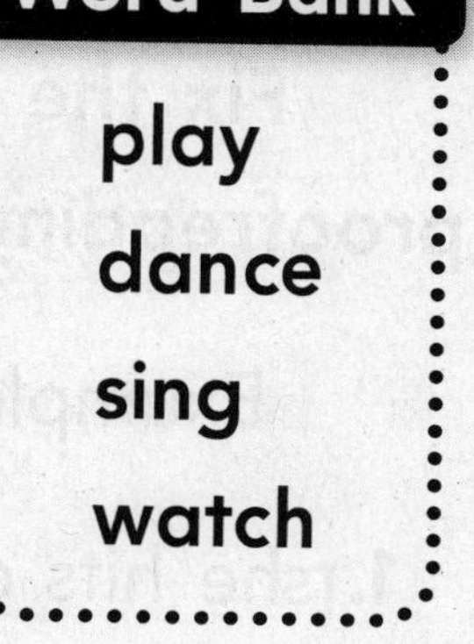

Word Bank

play
dance
sing
watch

1.  ______________________

2. ______________________

3.   ______________________

4.  ______________________

Name ______________________________

Grammar in Writing

A statement begins with a capital letter and ends with a period.

Fix the mistakes in these statements. Use proofreading marks.

Example: we play the bells.
(≡ under "w"; ∧ after "bells")

1. she hits a big drum
2. he holds a doll
3. they have big hats
4. we tap and sing

Proofreading Marks	
∧	add
≡	capital letter

Name ______________________

Words to Know

Circle the word that fits in each sentence. Write that word on the line.

1. I like to (read, after, was). ______

2. The cat (after, was, draw) in his bed. ______

3. I like to (after, was, draw) animals. ______

4. Here are (writes, pictures, reads) of my cat. ______

5. Now I will (was, after, write) to my dad. ______

6. I will help you (after, draw, read) I call Brad. ______

Name ______________________________

Clusters with *s*

Name each picture. Write the first two or three letters that stand for the beginning sounds. Use the letters from the box.

st	sw	sn	sk	str

1.  ______

2. 

______

3.  ______

4. 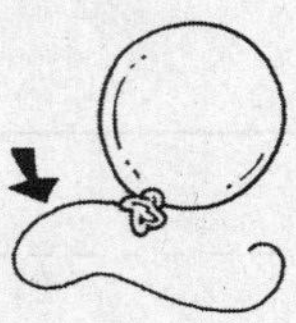 ______

5.  ______

Name ______________________________

Clusters with *s*

Circle the word that finishes the sentence. Write the word.

1.

Ann can __________ well.

spell swim

2.

Who made this __________?

spill snag

3.

I __________ in the tub.

sniff scrub

4.

This cat is not __________!

small scrap

5.

Pam likes to __________.

strum smell

6.

Kim will get a __________.

spin snack

Name ______________________

Spelling Words with the Short *e* Sound

Spelling Words

- yes
- let
- red
- ten
- bed
- get

Circle the word that names the picture. Then write the word.

1. bad
bed

____

2. ten
tan

____

Write the Spelling Words that rhyme with **wet**.

3. ______________________ **4.** ______________________

Proofread each sentence. Circle the Spelling Word that is wrong. Write it correctly.

5. I have a rud pen. ______________________

6. I said yez. ______________________

Name ____________________

Lesson 9
PRACTICE BOOK

Dr. Seuss
Grammar: Singular and Plural Nouns

One and More Than One

Listen to the nouns and read along. Circle the noun for each picture below. Then write the nouns you circled.

1.  bird birds ____________________

2.  boy boys ____________________

3. 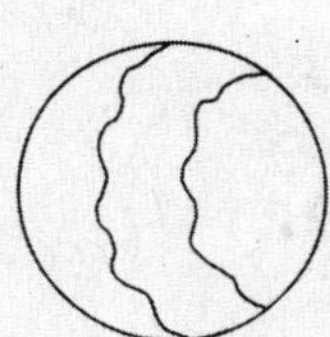 ball balls ____________________

4.  tree trees ____________________

5.   cake cakes ____________________

Name ______________________________

Telling How Things Look

Draw a picture of a make-believe animal.

one
two
three
four
blue
red
yellow
big
small
round

Finish the sentences that describe your animal. Listen to the words in the box. You can use these and other words you choose.

1. The ______________ looks ______________.

2. Its ______________ are ______________.

3. It has ______________ ______________.

Name ______________________________

Lesson 9
PRACTICE BOOK

Dr. Seuss
Phonics: Short *e* and Clusters with *s*

Short *e* and Clusters with *s*

Name each picture. Circle the letters that stand for the beginning sounds. Write the letters. Write the word.

1. 
st
sw ___ ___ i m ______________

2. 
ru
re ___ ___ s t ______________

3. 
st
sn ___ ___ a c k ______________

4. 
ve
ne ___ ___ s t ______________

5. 
fl
sl ___ ___ i p ______________

6. 
de
di ___ ___ s k ______________

Name ____

Text and Graphic Features

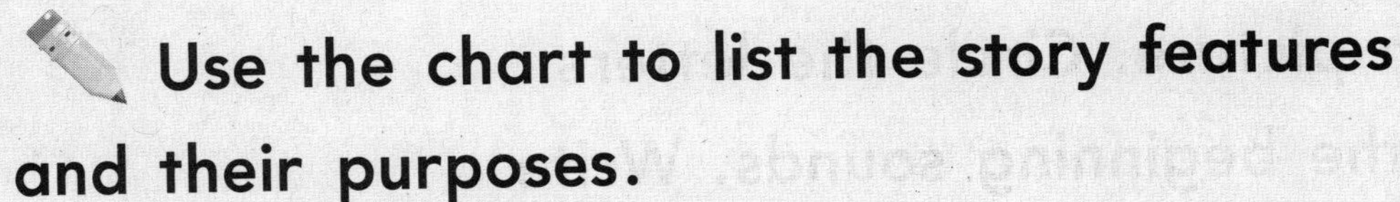

Use the chart to list the story features and their purposes.

Feature	Purpose

Name ____________________

Dr. Seuss
Spelling: Words with Short *e*

Spelling Words with the Short *e* Sound

Write the Spelling Words in ABC order.

1. ____________________
2. ____________________
3. ____________________
4. ____________________
5. ____________________
6. ____________________

Spelling Words

- yes
- let
- red
- ten
- bed
- get

Name ______________________________

Special Plural Nouns

Listen to the nouns and read along. Circle the noun for each picture below. Then write the nouns you circled.

1.  woman women ______________

2.  woman women ______________

3.  man men ______________

4.  man men ______________

5.  child children ______________

6.  child children ______________

Name ______________________________

Dr. Seuss
Spelling: Words with Short *e*

Spelling Words with the Short *e* Sound

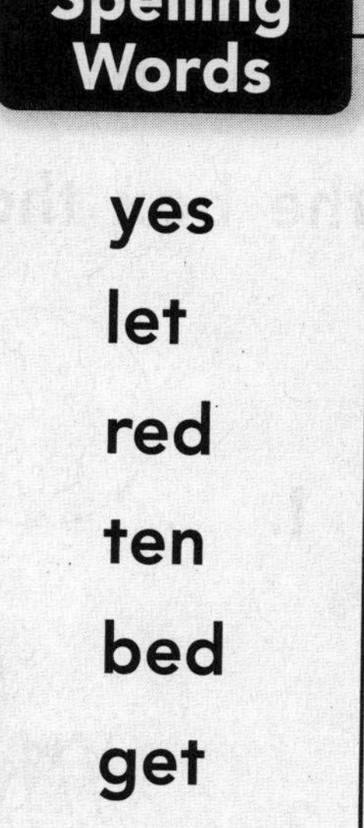

Write a Spelling Word to complete each sentence.

1. Get out of ____________, Fred!
2. Will you ____________ me in?
3. Ben has ____________ pet ducks.
4. Will you ____________ that bug away from me?
5. ____________, I will hop with you.
6. Jeff likes the ____________ cap best.

Name ______________________________

Spiral Review

Listen to the adjectives in the Word Bank. Read along. Write an adjective from the box that tells about each picture.

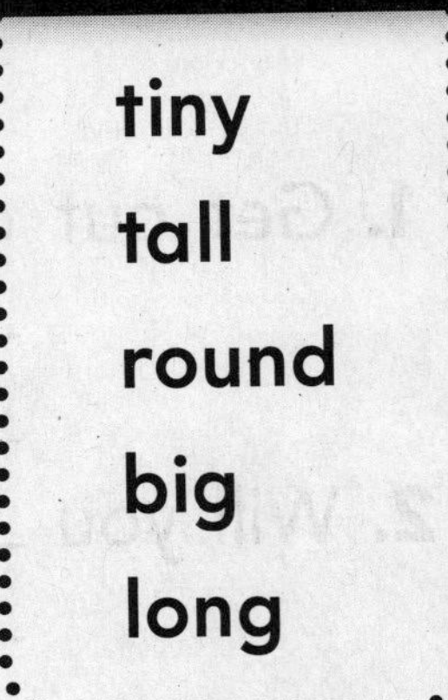

Word Bank

tiny
tall
round
big
long

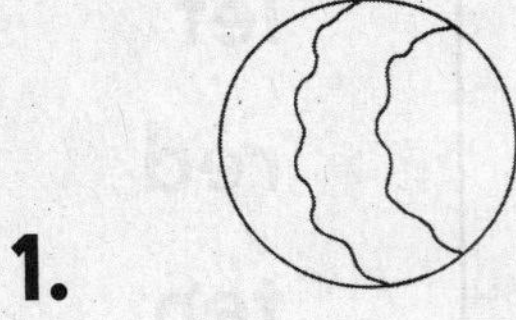

1. a ______________ ball

2. a ______________ ant

3. a ______________ man

4. a ______________ snake

5. a ______________ house

Name ________________________________

Planning My Description

Listen to the labels in the web and read along. Write and draw details that tell size, shape, color, and number.

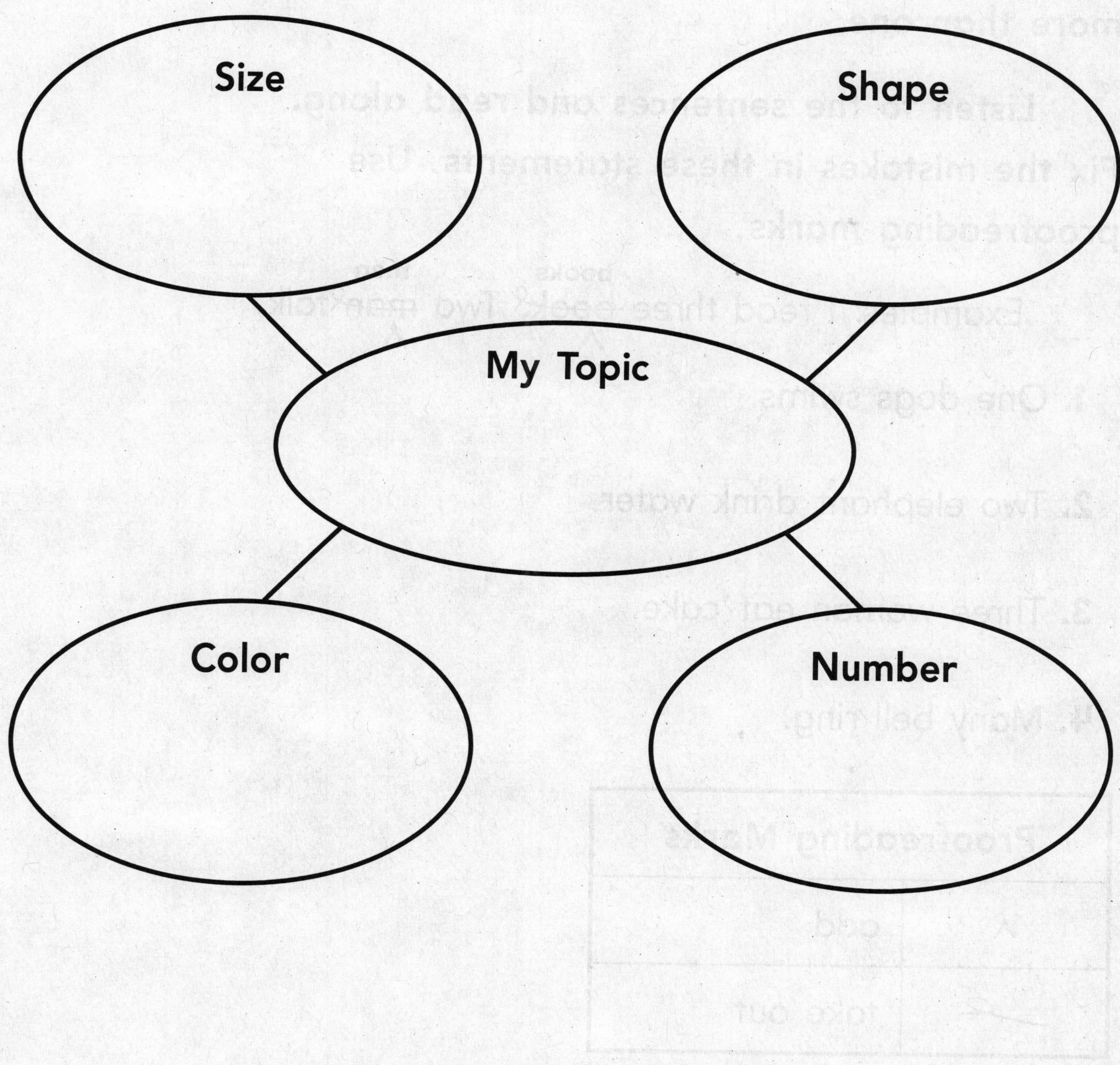

Name ______________________________

Grammar in Writing

Some nouns name one. Some nouns name more than one.

An s ending means more than one. Some special nouns change their spelling to name more than one.

Listen to the sentences and read along. Fix the mistakes in these statements. Use proofreading marks.

Examples: I read three ~~book~~ books. Two ~~man~~ men talk.

1. One dogs swims.

2. Two elephant drink water.

3. Three woman eat cake.

4. Many bell ring.

Proofreading Marks	
^	add
(delete mark)	take out

Name ______________________

Words to Know

Write a word from the box to complete each sentence. Use the leftover word to write a sentence.

Words to Know

eat	give	one
put	small	take

1. Liz will ______________ Ken a box.

2. He will ______________ a snack.

3. I can see ______________ duck.

4. The ant is ______________.

5. Jill will ______________ the truck away.

____

Name ______________________________

A Cupcake Party
Phonics: Final Clusters

Final Clusters

Name each picture. Write the letters that stand for the ending sounds. Use the letters from the box.

nd	mp	nt	st	sk

1. ____ ____

2. ____ ____

3. ____ ____

4. ____ ____

5. ____ ____

6. ____ ____

Name ______________________________

Final Clusters

Name each picture. Circle the word to finish the sentence.

1.

Fran has a ______.

list gift

2.

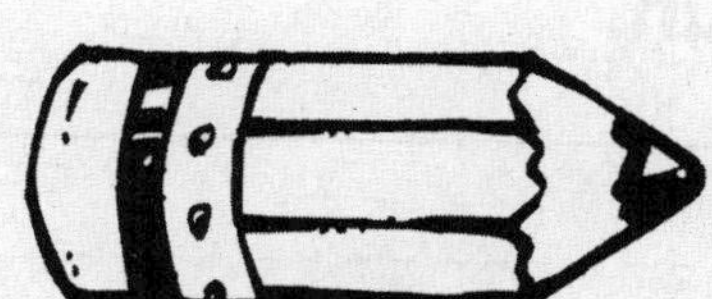

You can ______ with this.

grasp print

3.

Ann plays in the ______.

sand dust

4.

It can ______ up.

land jump

5.

Do you sit at a ______?

desk pond

6.

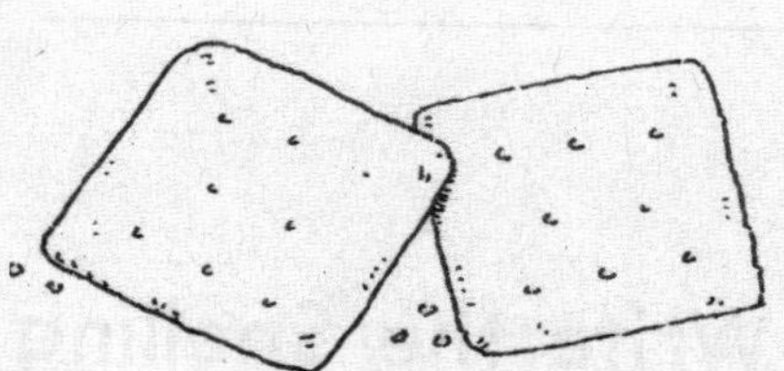

These can be very ______.

stand crisp

Name ________________________

Spelling Words with the Short *u* Sound

Spelling Words

- us
- sun
- but
- fun
- bus
- run

Write the Spelling Words that end with un.

1. ________________________

2. ________________________

3. ________________________

Write the Spelling Words that end with us.

4. ________________________

5. ________________________

Write the Spelling Word that ends with ut.

6. ________________________

Name ______________________

Prepositions for Where

A Cupcake Party
Grammar: Prepositions

Circle the preposition in each sentence. Write it on the line.

1. The gift was in a box. ______
2. Nan put it on a desk. ______
3. Some are under a bed. ______
4. The gift fell off the desk. ______

Complete each sentence. Write a preposition that tells where.

5. Nan went ______ the steps.
6. She put Dan's gift ______ the desk.

Name ______________________________

A Cupcake Party
Writing: Write to Describe

Writing a Topic Sentence

Look at the picture of Stan the Skunk. Tell what Stan looks like. Write a topic sentence and some details.

Topic Sentence: ______________________________

____

He has a ______________________________.

He has ______________________________.

Name ______________________

Short *u* and Final Clusters

Name each picture. Write the last two consonants that stand for the sounds at the end of the word. Choose consonants from the box.

lp	nt	mp	ft	sk

1. ju ______

2. a ______

3. he ______

4. so ______

5. bu ______

6. ma ______

Name ______________________________

Story Structure

A Cupcake Party
Comprehension: Story Structure

Use the Story Map to identify the characters, setting, and plot in the story.

Characters	Setting
Plot	

Name ______________________________

Spelling Words with the Short *u* Sound

Write the missing letter to complete each Spelling Word. Then write the word.

Spelling Words

us
sun
but
fun
bus
run

1. b ____ t ______________
2. s ____ n ______________
3. ____ s ______________
4. f ____ n ______________
5. b ____ s ______________
6. r ____ n ______________

Name ______________________

Prepositions for When

Listen to the prepositions in the word box. Read along. Circle the preposition in each sentence. Write it on the line.

during	at	after	before

1. Let us write after we read. ______________

2. We will sing during class. ______________

3. She will come back before you do. ______________

Complete each sentence. Write a preposition that tells when.

4. I read ______________ I go to bed.

5. We will go ______________ six.

Name ______________________________

Spelling Words with the Short *u* Sound

Write a Spelling Word to complete each sentence.

1. Here comes the ______________.

2. The ______________ is up.

3. The dog can ______________ fast.

Write the correct word to complete each sentence.

4. Will you come with ______________? **us** **is**

5. We had a lot of ______________. **fun** **fan**

6. I like black ______________ not red. **bat** **but**

Name ______________________

Spiral Review

Listen to the adjectives in the Word Bank. Read along. Write an adjective from the box that tells about each picture.

Word Bank

two
three
four

1.  ______________

2.  ______________

3. ______________

Listen to the adjectives in the Word Bank. Read along. Write an adjective from the box to finish the sentence.

Word Bank

green
blue

4. The sky is ______________ .

Name ___

Grammar in Writing

Write four sentences about the picture with prepositions that tell where or when. Draw a line under each preposition.

1. where ___

2. where ___

3. when ___

4. when ___

Name ______________________________

Words to Know

Listen to the riddles. Read along. Circle the best answer to each riddle.

1. This is a place that is not near.	**far**	**where**	**live**
2. This is how snow feels.	**their**	**blue**	**cold**
3. This word could start a question.	**far**	**where**	**live**
4. A rock does not do this.	**cold**	**where**	**live**
5. Rain is made of this.	**water**	**far**	**cold**
6. The sky is this.	**where**	**blue**	**little**
7. This is not big.	**water**	**little**	**far**
8. This belongs to more than one person.	**their**	**water**	**far**

Name ________________________________

Words with *th*

Circle the word that matches the picture.

1.

wind   with

2.

tan   thin

3.

them   ten

4.

bat   bath

5.

path   pet

6.

kick   thick

Name ________________________

Words with *th*

Write th to finish the word and read it.

Circle the picture that matches the word.

1.

1 + 1 = 2

ma ___ ___

2.

13

___ ___ink

3.

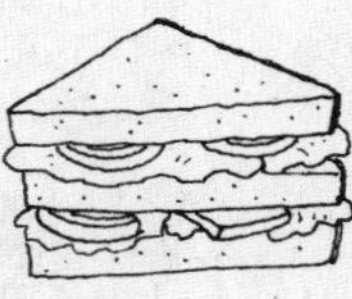

___ ___ick

4.

ba ___ ___

5.

___ ___is

Name ______________________________

Spelling Words with the *th* Sound

Sort the words. Write the correct Spelling Words in each column.

Words that begin with th	Words that end with th

Spelling Words

that
then
this
them
with
bath

Name ______________________________

Names for People and Animals

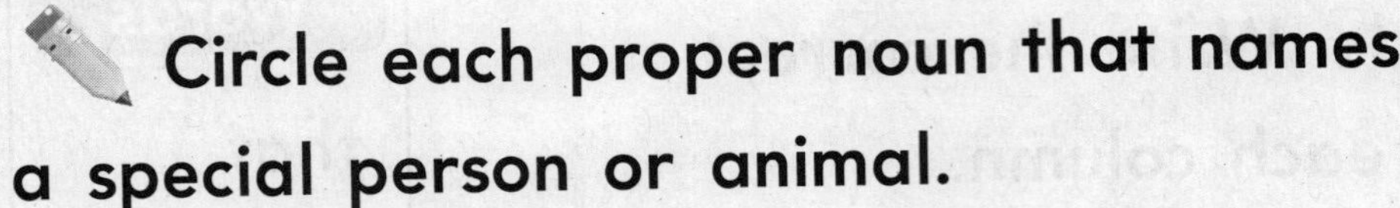

Circle each proper noun that names a special person or animal.

1. My friend Kim sees a crab.

2. Stan Bock sees it, too.

3. They call the crab Fred .

Draw a line under each proper noun that names a special person or animal. Then write the proper noun correctly.

4. ann smith jumps into the water.

____

5. Her friend fran sees a crab with spots.

____

6. She calls the crab spots.

____

Name ______________________________

Words That Tell How

 Draw a sea animal.

Word Bank

- softly
- loudly
- slowly
- quickly
- fast
- happily
- sadly
- sleepily
- gently

Write sentences about your animal. Listen to the words in the box. Use these words and other words you choose.

Sea Animal	Action Verb	How

Sea Animal	Action Verb	How

Name ______________________________

Sea Animals
Phonics: Base Words and *-s*, *-es*, *-ed*, *-ing*

Base Words and *-s*, *-es*, *-ed*, *-ing*

Read the sentences. Circle the sentence that tells about the picture.

1. The cat jumped.

   The cat sat.

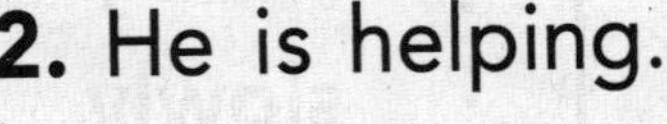

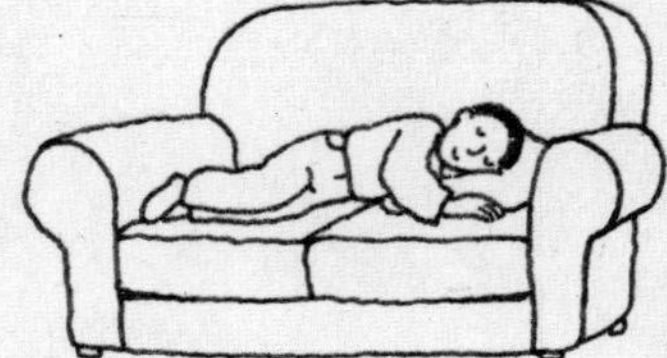

2. He is helping.

   He is resting.

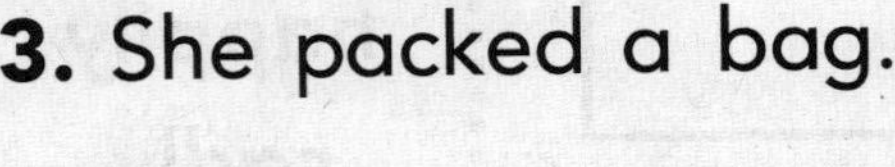

3. She packed a bag.

   She pulled a bag.

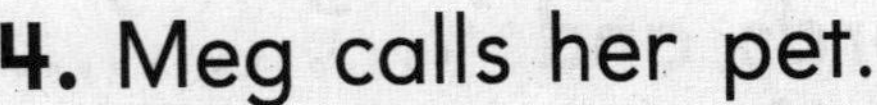

4. Meg calls her pet.

   Meg pets her cat.

5. Val is drawing.

   Val is looking.

Name ______________________________

Author's Purpose

Think about why the author wrote Sea Animals. Then write the author's purpose and three details that tell about the purpose.

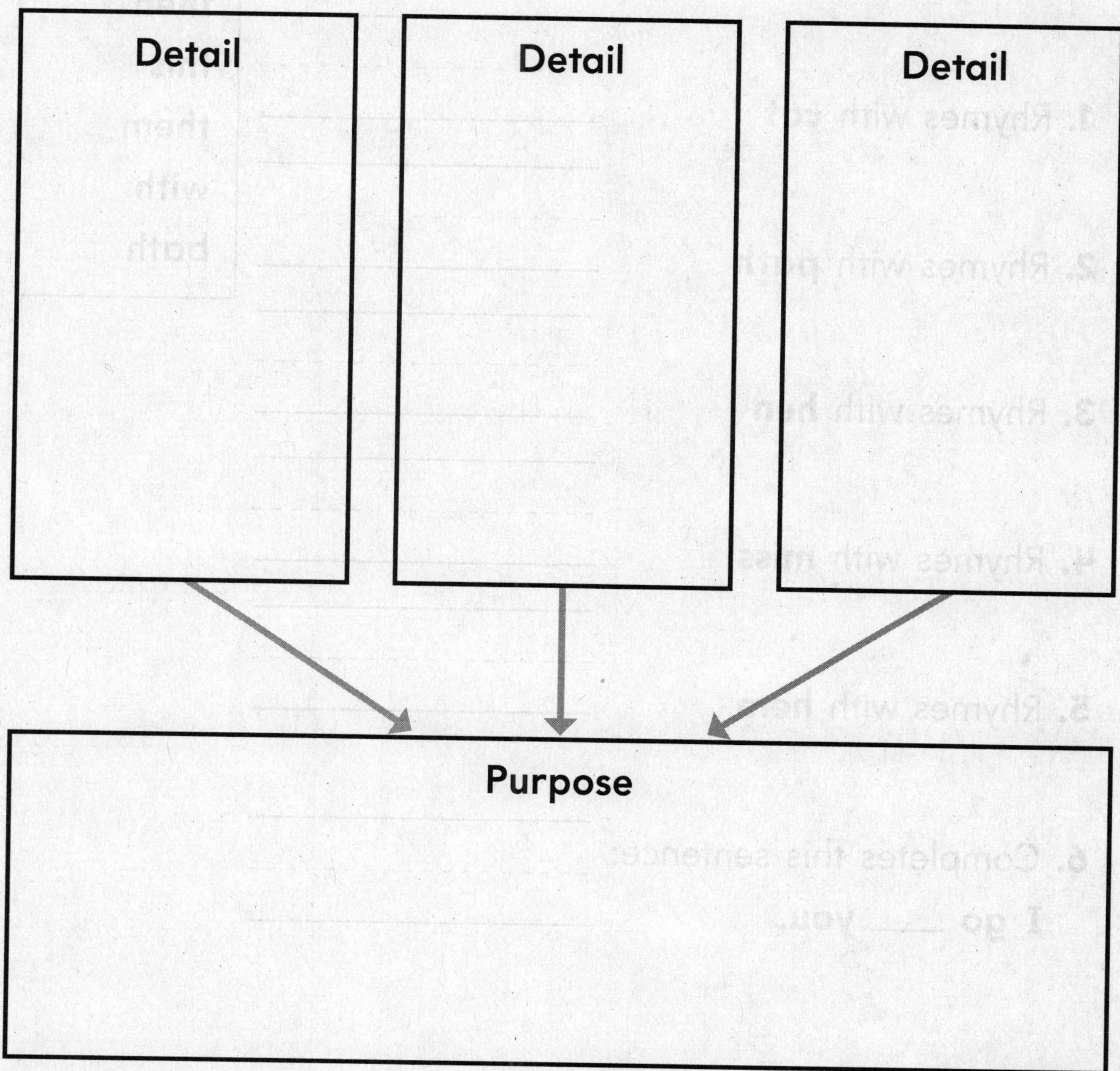

Name ______________________________

Sea Animals
Spelling: Words with *th*

Spelling Words with the *th* Sound

Listen to the clues. Read along. Write the Spelling Word that fits each clue.

Spelling Words

- that
- then
- this
- them
- with
- bath

1. Rhymes with **cat** ______________
2. Rhymes with **path** ______________
3. Rhymes with **hen** ______________
4. Rhymes with **miss** ______________
5. Rhymes with **hem** ______________
6. Completes this sentence: ______________
   I go ____ you.

Name ___________________________

Titles for People

Write the titles and names correctly.

1. mrs Scott ___________________________

2. mr Long ___________________________

Draw a line under each title. Then write the title and name correctly.

3. Today miss Hill will play the drums.

____

4. Can dr Well fix the dog's leg?

____

5. ms. Hass takes a picture of the class.

____

Name ______________________________

Planning My Sentences

 **Write and draw facts about your sea animal.**

My Topic

Fact 1

Fact 2

Name ______________________

Sea Animals
Spelling: Words with *th*

Spelling Words with the *th* Sound

Write a Spelling Word from the box to complete each sentence.

Spelling Words

that
bath
them

1. ____________ hat is for Jack.

2. Tell ____________ to come in now.

3. I like to give my dog a ____________.

Write a Spelling Word from the box to complete each sentence.

Spelling Words

then
this
with

4. ____________ Jon was up at bat.

5. Matt, is ____________ your hat?

6. Sam went swimming ____________ me.

Name ____________________

Spiral Review

Draw a line under each word group that is a sentence.

1. The friends play tag.

2. digs in the sand

3. The frog jumps up.

4. Some kids look for crabs.

5. A red fox

Write a group of words from each word box to make a sentence.

The crab This will	a rock rests on a rock

6. ____________________.

Name ___

Grammar in Writing

Nouns that name special people or animals are called **proper nouns**. Proper nouns begin with capital letters.

A **title** before a person's name begins with a capital letter. A title usually ends with a period.

Fix the mistakes in these statements. Use proofreading marks.

Examples: My fish is named gus.
I gave Mrs Billows a book.

1. My friend Dr Rudd helps animals.
2. He has a pet crab called pinch.
3. Our teacher, miss Land, reads about crabs.
4. She gives the book to beth Bond.

Proofreading Marks	
∧	add
≡	capital letter

Name ______________________________

Words to Know

Circle the word that best completes each sentence.

1. The dog is (brown, very).

2. Rich got the gift (been, out) of the box.

3. I would like to have my (never, own) cat.

4. Singing makes me (very, brown) happy.

5. Have you (know, been) to the play?

6. Do you (know, very) what to do next?

7. Take (off, never) that hat.

8. You (own, never) sing with me.

Name ___________________________

Words with *ch*, *tch*

Circle the word that matches the picture.

1.

thick chick

2.

chip champ

3.

bend bench

4.

hatch hut

5.

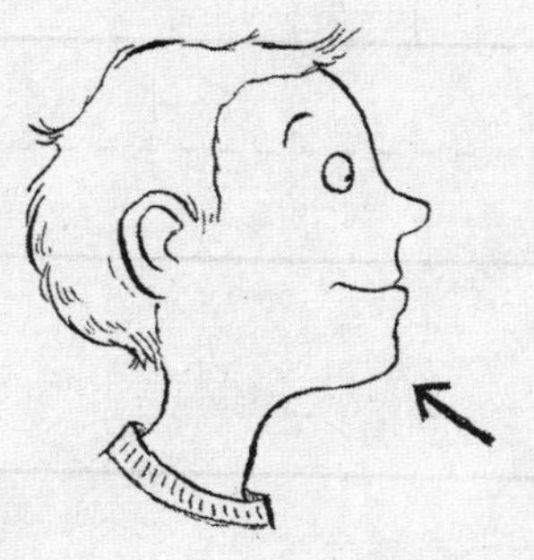

chin check

6.

cats catch

Name ______________________________

Words with *ch*, *tch*

Read the words in the box. Write the word that matches the picture.

Word Bank

lunch check chimp chop match

1. ______________________

2. ______________________

3. ______________________

4. ______________________

5. ______________________

Name ____________________

Spelling Words with the *ch* Sound

Sort the words. Write the correct Spelling Words in each column.

Words that begin with ch	Words that end with ch

Spelling Words

chin
chop
much
chip
rich
chick

Name ______________________________

Names of Places

Listen to some proper nouns in the Word Bank. Read along. Circle each proper noun that names a special place in the sentences.

Word Bank

Street	Avenue	Park	Lake	School

1. There are many animals in Red Fox Park.
2. I live on Mint Avenue.
3. It is near Elk Street.

Draw a line under each proper noun that names a special place. Then write the proper noun correctly.

4. We camp at elm lake.

____

5. My friend lives on crab avenue.

____

Name ______________________________

Order Words

Write 1, 2, and 3 to put these pictures in order.

Write instructions that tell how to feed a cat. Use order words.

Order Word	Action	Thing
Order Word	**Action**	**Thing**
Order Word	**Action**	**Thing**

Name ________________________________

Possessives with *'s*

Read the sentences. Circle the sentence that tells about the picture.

1. Mom's hat is off!

   Dad's hat is wet.

2. My cat's leg is cut.

   My cat's bed is small.

3. Meg's bag is big.

   Peg's bag is little.

4. Tim's picture is cold.

   Tom's picture is funny.

5. My pal's pet is wet.

   The vet is my pet's friend.

Name ____________________

Sequence of Events

Use the chart to tell the sequence of events in the story.

First

Next

Last

Name ______________________________

Spelling Words with *ch*

Listen to the clues. Read along. Write the Spelling Word that fits each clue.

Spelling Words

chin
chop
much
chip
rich
chick

1. Opposite of **poor** ______________
2. Rhymes with **hop** ______________
3. Rhymes with **fin** ______________
4. Opposite of **little** ______________
5. Rhymes with **hip** ______________
6. Rhymes with **kick** ______________

Name ______________________________

More Place Names

Circle each proper noun that names a special place.

1. Frank went to see Bill in Kansas.

2. Bill just got back from Canada.

Draw a line under each proper noun that names a special place. Then write the proper noun correctly.

3. It is very cold in finland.

____

4. Meg lives in dallas.

____

5. That is in texas.

____

Name ____________________

Planning My Instructions

Write steps for making an animal puppet. Write the steps in order. Use an order word for each step.

My Topic: How to ____________________

1. ____________________

2. ____________________

3. ____________________

4. ____________________

Name ______________________

Spelling Words with the *ch* Sound

Write the correct word to complete each sentence.

1. Jan rubs her ______________ .
2. The ______________ is small and soft.
3. How ______________ does it cost?
4. Dad will ______________ the nuts.
5. There is a ______________ in the cup.
6. The king was very ______________ .

chin
fin

chick
check

chum
much

chop
chat

ship
chip

rich
rip

Name ______________________________

Spiral Review

Listen to the animal names in the Word Bank. Read along. Draw lines to match naming parts and action parts. Your sentence should tell about the picture.

Word Bank

zebras giraffe turtle

1. The zebras	is hot.
2. A giraffe	drink water.
3. The turtle	has a snack.
4. The sun	takes a swim.

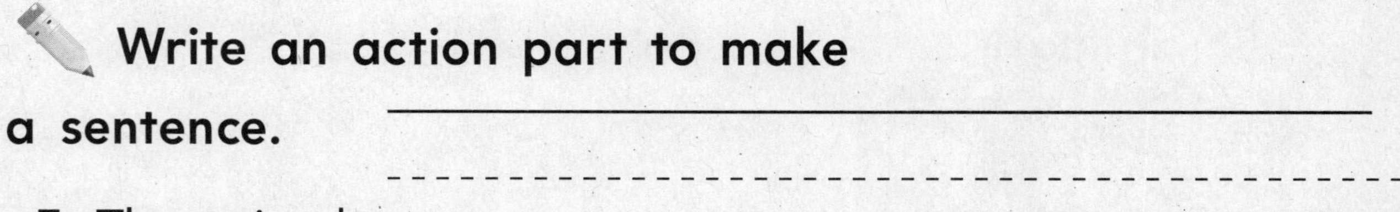

Write an action part to make a sentence.

5. The animals ______________________________.

Name ______________________________

Grammar in Writing

Proper nouns name special places. They begin with capital letters. Listen to the nouns in the Word Bank. Read along. Some of these can be both proper and common nouns, such as **road.**

Word Bank

America School Road Canada

Fix the mistakes in these sentences. Use proofreading marks.

Example: We live in america.
≡ (under the "a" of america)

1. I go to red plum school.
2. I get on the bus at smith road.
3. Liz wants to see the grand canyon.
4. Have you been to canada?

Proofreading Marks	
≡	capital letter

Name ______________________________________

Seasons
High-Frequency Words

Words to Know

Circle the word that best completes each sentence.

1. Some frogs are (green, grow).

2. Let us have lunch (yellow, down) by the pond.

3. It gets cold in the (fall, new).

4. My plants will (down, grow) well in the sun.

5. Some of the buds are (goes, open).

6. Do you like my (new, down) hat?

7. A big (yellow, fall) truck will take the logs away.

8. The truck (green, goes) to the dump.

Name ___________________________________

Words with *sh*, *wh*, *ph*

Circle the word that matches the picture or belongs in the sentence.

1.

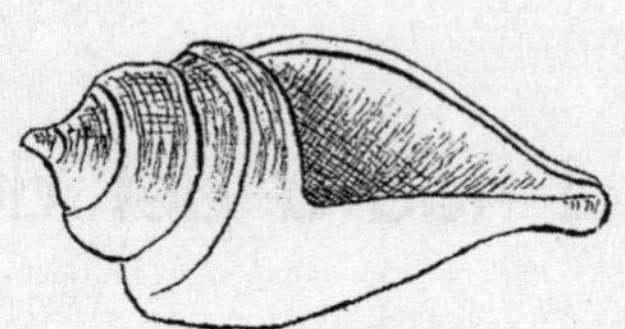

shell bell

2.

__________ is this?

What Wish

3.

__________ will he go?

Well When

4.

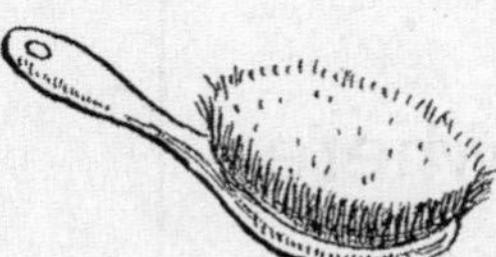

bunch brush

5.

fish fist

6.

Ralph Jen

Name ____________________

Words with *sh*, *wh*, *ph*

Circle the word that finishes the sentence. Then write the word on the line.

1.	wish witch	I ____________ I had a pet dog.
2.	pin ship	The ____________ was in the water.
3.	where her	Do you know ____________ she is?
4.	Then When	____________ will the shop open?
5.	tan graph	Dan will draw a math ____________ .

Name ______________________

Seasons
Spelling: Words with *sh* and *wh*

Spelling Words with the *sh* and *wh* Sounds

Spelling Words

ship
shop
which
when
whip
fish

Sort the words. Write the correct Spelling Words in each column.

Words with sh	Words with wh

Write two words that rhyme with lip.

_______________ _______________

Name ____________________

Subjects and Verbs

Write a verb from the box to tell what the underlined subject is doing.

Word Bank

- picks
- hops
- sits
- runs
- comes

1. The <u>sun</u> ____________ up.

2. <u>Bev</u> ____________ on the sand.

3. <u>Tim</u> ____________ up a stick.

4. A <u>frog</u> ____________ past.

5. A <u>dog</u> ____________ after the rabbits.

Name ____________________

Seasons
Writing: Write to Inform

Main Idea

Write facts to finish three sentences about a season. Then tell the main idea.

Topic Sentence

Here are some facts about ____________.

Detail Sentence

____________ is a time when ____________
____________________________________.

Detail Sentence

The weather in ____________ gets
____________________________________.

Main Idea

All my sentences tell about ____________.

Name ____________________

Seasons
Phonics: Contractions with *'s, n't*

Contractions with *'s, n't*

Draw a line from each pair of words to its contraction.

can not	don't
Let us	It's
do not	can't
It is	Let's

Write the contraction from above that finishes each sentence.

1. They ____________ know what to do.

2. ____________ good to help a friend.

3. ____________ go to see a play.

4. He ____________ find his hat.

Name ____________________

Cause and Effect

Use the chart to tell about causes and effects in Seasons.

What Happened?	Why Did It Happen?

Name ______________________________

Seasons
Spelling: Words with *sh* and *wh*

Spelling Words with the *sh* and *wh* Sounds

Spelling Words

ship
shop
which
when
whip
fish

Write sh or wh to complete each Spelling Word.

1\. 

___ ___ i p

2\. 

f i ___ ___

3\. 

___ ___ o p

4\. 

___ ___ i c h

5\. January

Sunday	Monday	Tuesday	Wednesday	Thursday	Friday	Saturday
			1	2	3	4
			8			
						18
19		21		23		
			29		31	

___ ___ e n

6\. 

___ ___ i p

Name ______________________________

Verbs with *s*

Listen to the nouns in the Word Bank and read along. Choose the correct verb to agree with the underlined subject. Write the verb to finish each sentence.

Word Bank

children boy girls

1. Many children ______________ by the pond.

   play plays

2. A boy ______________ in the water.

   jump jumps

3. The girls ______________ a ball.

   toss tosses

4. A boy and a dog ______________ on the sand.

   run runs

Name ________________________________

Seasons
Writing: Write to Inform

Planning My Sentences

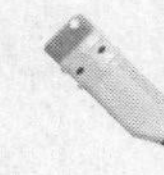

Choose a season. Then write facts about the season.

My Topic: ________________________________

Fact 1

Fact 2

Fact 3

Name ____________________

Spelling Words with *sh*, *wh*, *ph*

Write the correct word to complete each sentence.

1. The ______________ has left. (shell, ship, chip)

2. ______________ way did he go? (Which, Why, Who)

3. The ______________ sells hats. (chop, shop, she)

4. ______________ will you go? (Where, Went, When)

5. Can you ______________ the eggs? (win, why, whip)

6. The ______________ are yellow. (dash, fish, dish)

Name ______________________________

Spiral Review

Draw lines to match naming parts and action parts. Read the statements you made about the picture.

1. Jill	waters the plants.
2. Fred	takes a nap.
3. The mom	digs in the mud.
4. The dad	is looking.
5. The cat	holds a box of plants.

Name ______________________________

Grammar in Writing

- Add **s** to a **verb** when it tells about a noun that names one.
- Do not add **s** to a verb when it tells about a noun that names more than one.

Fix the mistakes in these sentences. Use proofreading marks.

Examples: Snowflakes ~~falls~~ **fall** on the ground.
David ~~put~~ **puts** on his coat.

1. Don get his sled.

2. Jan and Nick plays in the sand.

3. Nick make a hill of sand.

4. The dog jump in the grass.

5. Deb and Don finds a cat.

Proofreading Marks	
∧	add
___ ⸗	take out

Name ______________________________

Words to Know

Circle the word that best completes each sentence.

1. Can you (watch/into) my fish for me?

2. I will go (into/starts) class with you.

3. I am glad that lunch (watch/starts) at one.

4. The fox jumps (over/watch) the log.

Write the word for each number.

Words to Know

five
four
three
two

2 ______________________

3 ______________________

4 ______________________

5 ______________________

Name ______________________________________

Words with Long *a*

Circle the word that matches the picture.

1.

camp crane

2.

plane plan

3.

crack cake

4.

grass gate

5.

whale what

6.

vest vase

Name ____________________

Words with Long *a*

Write the word that goes with each clue.

Word Bank

plate
tape
male
skates
game
grape

1. You use this to close a box. ____________________

2. A man is this. ____________________

3. You eat from this. ____________________

4. Go fast on these. ____________________

5. This is little and can be green. ____________________

6. You play this with a friend. ____________________

Name ____________________

Spelling Words with the Long *a* Sound

Write the Spelling Words in ABC order.

Spelling Words

came
make
brave
late
gave
shape

Name ____________________

Verbs with *ed*

Circle the verbs that tell about the past. Write those verbs.

1. The game ____________ at one.

starts **started**

2. Stan ____________ the box.

fills **filled**

3. Jane ____________ at the pictures.

looks **looked**

4. The frog ____________ very far.

jumps **jumped**

5. Mr. Scott ____________ the best one.

picks **picked**

Name ______________________________

Taking Notes

Listen to this passage about camels. Read along.

Many camels live in deserts. Camels have long legs and humps on their backs. Camels can live to be 50 or even 60 years old. Camels eat plants that grow in the desert.

Take notes about camels. Use words and pictures. Put your notes in the correct boxes.

Bodies

How Long They Live

Food

Name ______________________________

Words with Soft *c, g, dge*

Write the word from the box that rhymes with the set of words.

Word Bank

face
gem
page
cell
judge
wedge

1. fudge nudge budge ______________

2. cage wage rage ______________

3. race lace pace ______________

4. them hem stem ______________

5. tell bell yell ______________

6. edge ledge hedge ______________

Name ________________________________

Conclusions

Write three story details about Red Lizard and the race. Then write a conclusion telling how you think Red Lizard feels at the end of the story.

Detail	Detail	Detail

Conclusion

Name ______________________________

Spelling Words with the Long *a* Sound

Listen to the clues. Read along. Write the Spelling Word that fits each clue.

Spelling Words

came
make
brave
late
gave
shape

1. Rhymes with **tape** ______________
2. Opposite of **afraid** ______________
3. Rhymes with **gate** ______________
4. Rhymes with **tame** ______________
5. Rhymes with **cave** ______________
6. Rhymes with **bake** ______________

Present and Past Time

Listen to the time words in the Word Bank. Read along. Circle the correct verb to show present or past time. Write it on the line.

Word Bank

now today yesterday

1. Meg ______________ at the clock now. (present time)

looks **looked**

2. Today we ______________ games for math. (present time)

play **played**

3. Yesterday Ron ______________ his dad make lunch. (past time)

help **helped**

Name ______________________

Spelling Words with the Long *a* Sound

Spelling Words

came
late
make
brave
shape
gave

Write a Spelling Word from the box to complete each sentence.

1. I got here ______________ .

2. Will you ______________ me a cake?

3. He ______________ to play with me.

4. Max is big and ______________ .

5. He ______________ me a new pen.

6. What ______________ is that box?

Name ______________________________

Spiral Review

Listen to the nouns. Read along. Circle the correct noun to name each picture. Then write the noun.

1. prize prizes ______________

2. child children ______________

3. plant plants ______________

4.  woman women ______________

Finish the sentence with the correct word.

5. Many ______________ ran in the race.

animal animals

Name ______________________________

Planning My Report

Write a question about the animal you choose. Then find and write facts to answer your question.

My Topic: ______________________________

My Question

Fact 1

Fact 2

Fact 3

Name ______________________________

Grammar in Writing

- Some verbs tell what is happening now. Some verbs tell what happened in the past.
- Add **ed** to most verbs to tell about the past.

Listen to the time words in the Word Bank. Read along. Fix the mistakes in these sentences. Use proofreading marks.

Word Bank

now **yesterday** **last night**

Example: Many people ~~watch~~ ^watched the race last night.

1. The animals played now.

2. The frog and snake talk yesterday.

3. Last night the rat visits the duck.

Proofreading Marks	
^	add
~~—~~	take out

Name ______________________________

Words to Know

Circle the correct word to complete each sentence.

1. Lan goes for a (walk, bird) in the park.

2. It is a very (both, long) path.

3. Lan sees a (or, bird) in its nest.

4. Will it (fly, long) away when it sees her?

5. Two ducks in the lake are (bird, both) wet.

6. Their (eyes, walk) are black.

7. Lan likes to watch (those, eyes) ducks.

8. Lan has to go now (fly, or) she will be late.

Name ______________________________

Animal Groups
Phonics: Words with Long *i*

Words with Long *i*

Circle the word that matches the picture.

1\.

bake bike

2\.

dime dim

3\.

print prize

4\.

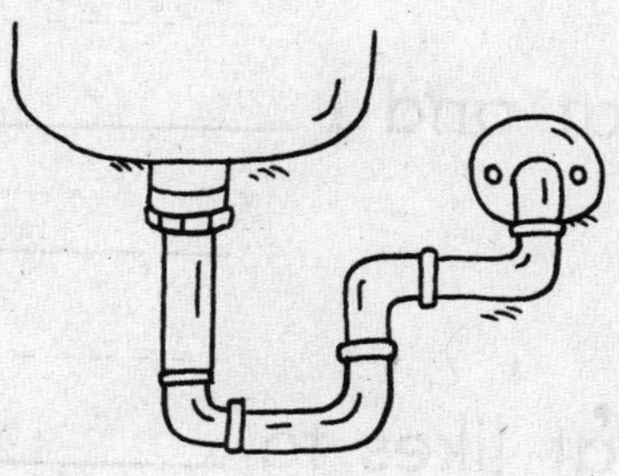

pale pipe

5\.

miss mice

6\.

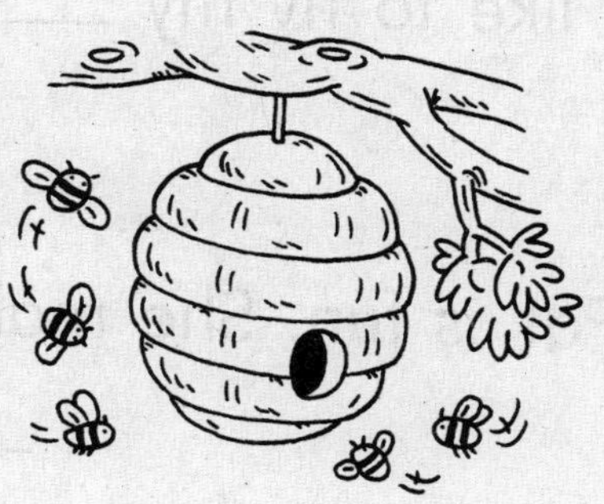

hive have

Name ______________________

Words with Long *i*

Write the word that best completes each sentence. Use words from the Word Bank.

Word Bank

time
smile
ride
like
kite

1. Pat and I ______________ to play.

2. Pat likes to ______________ her bike.

3. I like to fly my ______________.

4. Pat is fun. She makes me ______________.

5. We have a good ______________.

Name ____________________

Animal Groups
Spelling: Words with Long *i*

Spelling Words with the Long *i* Sound

Look at the picture. Write the missing letter to complete each Spelling Word.

Spelling Words

drive
time
bike
white
kite
like

1.

t ___ m e

2.

l ___ k e

3.

k ___ t e

4.

b ___ k e

5.

w h ___ t e

6.

d r ___ v e

Name ______________________________

Animal Groups
Grammar: The Verb *be*

Using *is* and *are*

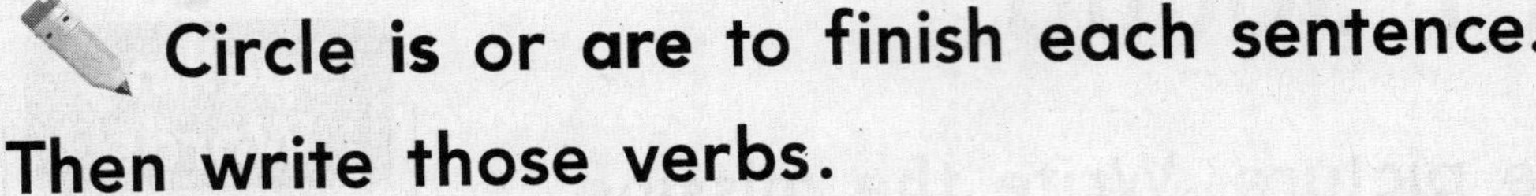

Circle is or are to finish each sentence. Then write those verbs.

1. The eyes ______________ blue.

   is **are**

2. The snake ______________ thin.

   is **are**

3. The chicks ______________ soft.

   is **are**

4. The mice ______________ very little.

   is **are**

5. The egg ______________ small.

   is **are**

Name ______________________________

Using Clear Words

Animal Groups
Writing: Write to Inform

Listen to the animal names. Read along. Make the meaning of each sentence clearer. Write new words to take the place of the underlined word or words.

1.	A giraffe is big. A giraffe is ______________________________.
2.	Puppies can play. Puppies can ______________________________.
3.	Squirrels can go up tall things. Squirrels can go up ______________________________.

Name ____________________

Digraphs *kn*, *wr*, *gn*, *mb*

Circle the two words in each row that begin or end with the same sound. Write the letters that spell the sound.

kn   wr   gn   mb

1.	wrap white wrist	___ ___
2.	lamb numb crab	___ ___
3.	kite knot knack	___ ___
4.	grape gnash gnat	___ ___
5.	write water wren	___ ___
6.	knife knit kick	___ ___

Name ____________________

Compare and Contrast

Animal Groups
Comprehension: Compare and Contrast

Write things about birds in the first oval. Write things about mammals in the other oval. Then write things about both of them where the ovals connect.

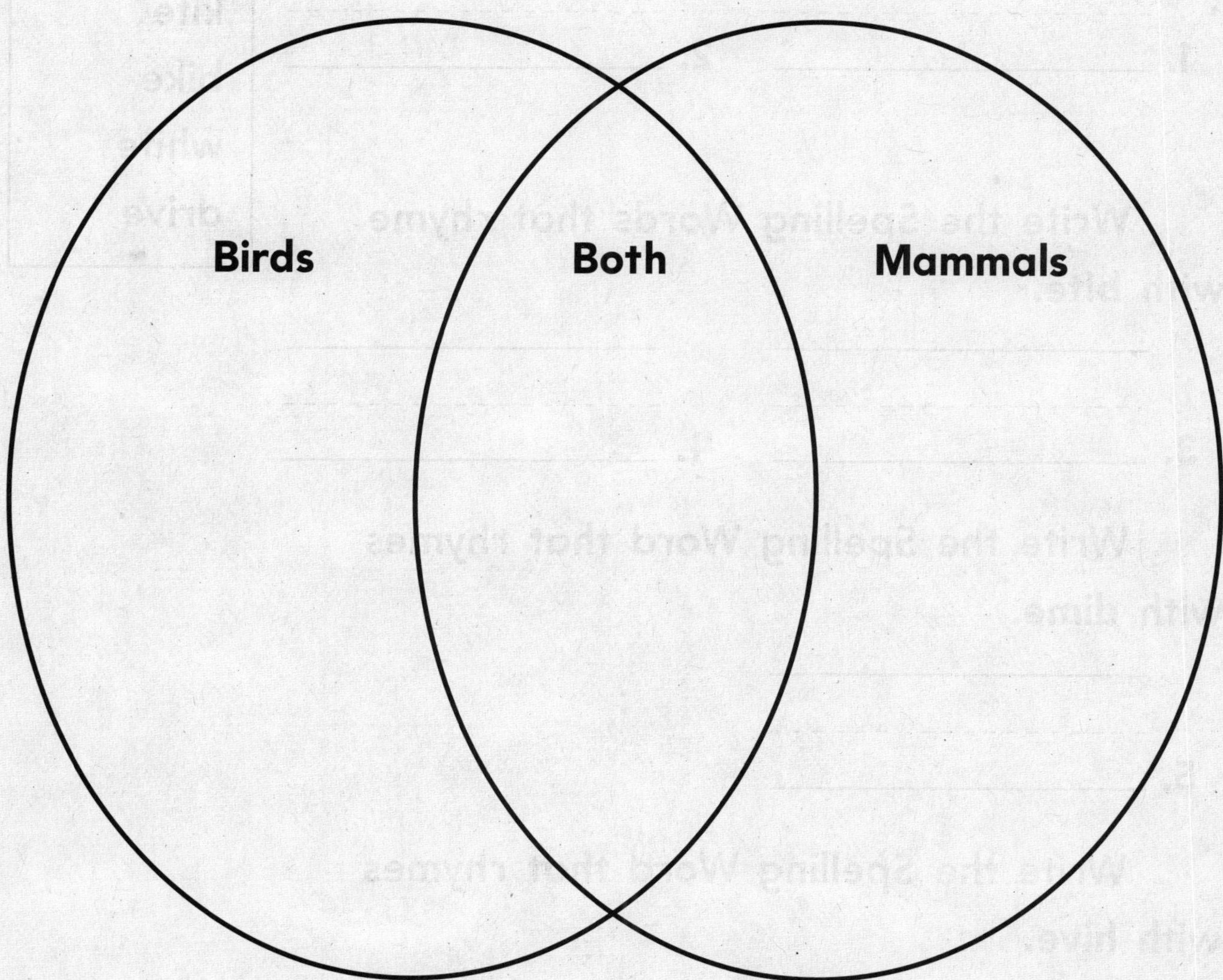

Name ______________________

Animal Groups
Spelling: Words with Long *i*

Spelling Words with the Long *i* Sound

Spelling Words

- time
- like
- kite
- bike
- white
- drive

Write the Spelling Words that rhyme with hike.

1. ______________ 2. ______________

Write the Spelling Words that rhyme with bite.

3. ______________ 4. ______________

Write the Spelling Word that rhymes with dime.

5. ______________

Write the Spelling Word that rhymes with hive.

6. ______________

Name ______________________________

Using *was* and *were*

Circle was or were to finish each sentence. Then write the verb on the line.

1. The cat ____________ napping.

was **were**

2. The ducks ____________ in the pond.

was **were**

3. The pigs ____________ in their pen.

was **were**

4. The snake ____________ on the grass.

was **were**

5. The frogs ____________ in the water.

was **were**

Name ______________________________

Spelling Words with the Long *i* Sound

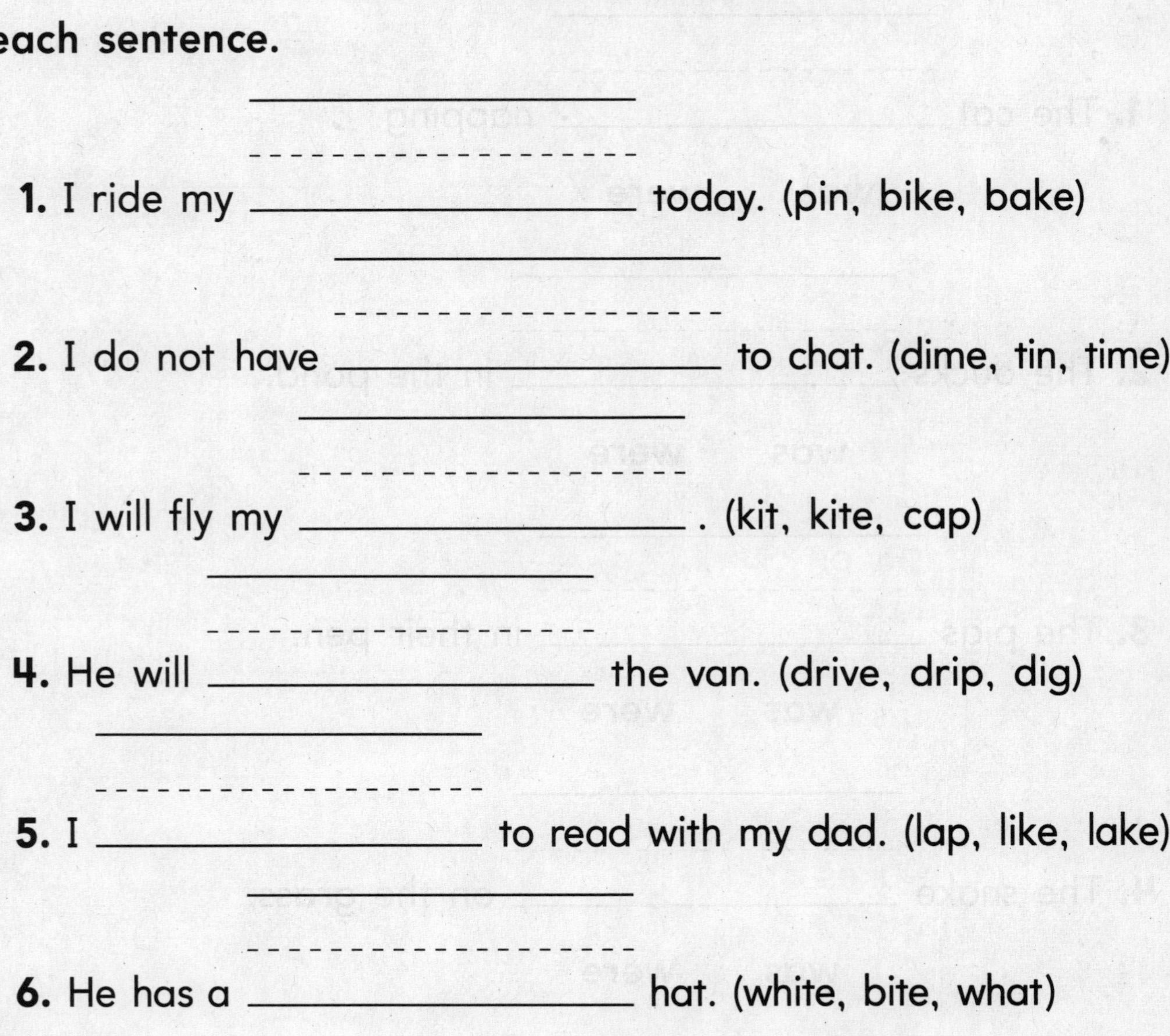

Write the correct word to complete each sentence.

1. I ride my ____________ today. (pin, bike, bake)

2. I do not have ____________ to chat. (dime, tin, time)

3. I will fly my ____________ . (kit, kite, cap)

4. He will ____________ the van. (drive, drip, dig)

5. I ____________ to read with my dad. (lap, like, lake)

6. He has a ____________ hat. (white, bite, what)

Name ____________________

Spiral Review

Circle the preposition in each sentence. Decide if the preposition tells where or when. Write where or when on the line.

1. Fish swim in the lake. ____________

2. The pup drinks after its mom has a drink. ____________

3. The frog sits on a rock. ____________

4. The fox runs up a hill. ____________

5. The dog wakes at five. ____________

6. Ducks fly over the pond. ____________

Name ______________________________

Grammar in Writing

- The verbs **is** and **are** tell what is happening now. The verbs **was** and **were** tell what happened in the past.
- Use **is** or **was** with a noun that names one.

Fix the mistakes in these sentences. Use proofreading marks.

Example: Frogs ~~was~~ **were** once tadpoles. A frog ~~are~~ **is** small.

1. Cats is mammals.

2. Dogs was once pups.

3. The fox were once a cub.

4. Apes is strong.

Proofreading Marks	
^	add
—ᵍ	take out